CHRISTOPHER CENTER

BASIC GUIDE

TO

FAMILY CHILD CARE

RECORD KEEPING

Fourth Edition

BY

TOM COPELAND

Redleaf Press
a division of Resources for Child Caring

Published by: Redleaf Press
Formerly Toys 'n Things Press
a division of Resources for Child Caring, Inc.
450 North Syndicate, Suite 5
St. Paul, MN 55104

Printed in the United States of America.

ISBN: 0-934140-89-8

Library of Congress Cataloging-in-Publication Data

Copeland, Tom.
    Basic guide to family child care record keeping / by Tom
Copeland. -- 4th ed.
        p.   cm.
    Rev. ed. of: Basic guide to family day care record keeping. c1988.
    ISBN 0-934140-89-8: $7.95
    1. Family day care—United States—Accounting.   2. Family day
care—Taxation—United States—Accounting. I. Copeland, Tom. Basic
guide to family day care record keeping. II. Title.
HF5686.F28C67   1992
362.7'12'068—dc20   92-34023
                                                       CIP

DISCLAIMER

The goal of this publication is to provide accurate information regarding federal tax record keeping for family child care providers. Despite our attempts to explain the tax laws in a simple manner, errors and omissions may occur in this text. Tax laws are in a constant state of change. We are selling this publication with the understanding that Redleaf Press and the author are not engaged in rendering legal, accounting, or other professional services. If legal or expert tax assistance is required, the services of a qualified professional should be obtained. This edition was based upon tax law as of June 30, 1993.

ACKNOWLEDGMENTS

I wish to gratefully acknowledge the many individuals who have worked on earlier editions of this publication, with special thanks to Deb Fish and Jean Nicol Jahren. I want to thank Linda Rodkewich, CPA; Brian Obermeier, CPA; R.M. Drierzynski, EA; Sandy Schroeder, EA; and John Czerwonka, CPA, for helping to clarify, for this edition, many record keeping issues in my discussions with them. I also want to thank record keeping and tax specialists Carrie M. Campbell, Lake V. Richart II, and Don Gilbo, and Carmela Pagnoni of "Cammie's Family Day Care" for reviewing this edition of the book and giving me their valuable feedback. Finally, I wish to thank Kristine Vesley for her copy editing, Alicia Raffel and Art Sidner for their design and typesetting, and Eileen Nelson for her editing and support through all the revisions of this edition. Any errors in this book, however, are my responsibility.

About The Author

Tom Copeland, the Family Child Care Business Specialist at Resources for Child Caring in St. Paul, Minnesota, has a law degree and has conducted record keeping, tax preparation, and business workshops for family child care providers across the country for eleven years. He is the author of *The Family Child Care Tax Workbook, Family Child Care Contracts and Policies: How to be Businesslike in a Caring Profession,* and *Successful Strategies for Recruiting Family Day Care Providers.* In addition, Tom writes a regular column on business issues in *Family Day Caring* magazine.

In 1988 Tom joined others in successfully lobbying the IRS to change its narrow interpretation of the business meal deduction rule that would have restricted providers to claiming only 80% of their food expenses. The IRS now allows providers to deduct 100% of their business food costs.

In 1991 Tom initiated a national campaign to reverse an IRS memorandum that would have required providers to keep track of how many hours each room in their home was used for their business. If the memo had been allowed to stand, it would have increased providers' record keeping responsibilities and decreased most providers' Time-Space percentages. Because of pressure from Congress and providers across the country, this memo was overturned in an IRS Revenue Ruling 92-3 published in January 1992 (See page 131 for a copy of the Ruling).

Redleaf National Institute

Redleaf Press and Resources for Child Caring have established a new service for family child care providers and organizations who work with providers such as Child Care Resource and Referral agencies, Child and Adult Care Food Programs, provider associations, and others. It is called the Redleaf National Institute.

The mission of the Institute is to provide accurate, understandable information on family child care business issues such as record keeping, tax preparation, contracts and policies, and legal matters. We will be publishing new books, offering provider training, teaching others to train providers, advocating on behalf of providers with the IRS and Congress, and offering other support services. It is our hope that we will be able to improve caregiving skills among providers across the country by helping them to take care of their business.

As the leading expert on family child care business issues in the country, Tom Copeland is conducting training sessions across the country for both providers and those who train providers. He is available to conduct training on a variety of topics in your area. For further information contact Resources for Child Caring, 450 North Syndicate Ave, Suite 5, St. Paul, MN 55104 or call 612-641-6675.

CONTENTS

A WORD ABOUT THIS BOOK

This guidebook was written specifically for those who care for children in their homes and get paid for it. Many providers are paying more in federal taxes than is necessary, because they are not keeping careful track of their expense deductions. They fail to keep track of their deductions either because they think it is too much work or because they don't know which expenses they can deduct. This book addresses both problems by explaining record keeping in a simple manner and by identifying hundreds of business deductions. The information in this book applies to providers in every state in the country, regardless of local regulations. Providers who do pay close attention to the recommendations in this book will be able to claim the maximum allowable deductions and pay the lowest possible taxes. Only federal tax rules are covered. I advise providers to consult their own state tax laws for additional regulations that may affect them.

HOW TO USE THE *BASIC GUIDE*

This book can be used most effectively as part of the series of business publications designed specifically for family child care providers by Redleaf Press. Although they may be purchased and read separately, used together they offer the provider the benefits of a powerful record keeping and tax preparation system.

These publications include:

Calendar-Keeper: A Record Keeping System for Child Care Providers. An annual calendar that helps providers organize their monthly attendance records, parent payments, Food Program income, business expenses, mileage records, and much more. May be presented to your tax preparer or at an IRS audit to support your business deductions.

Basic Guide to Family Child Care Record Keeping. A guidebook that tells providers *what* they can deduct for their business and *how* they can keep accurate records to support their deductions. Especially useful to new providers. Updated every few years.

Family Child Care Tax Workbook. This book identifies annual changes in the tax law and explains how to fill out the tax forms for the current year. A new edition is published in the late fall of each year. It describes how to fill out all the federal tax forms for your business, including **Schedule C: Profit or Loss From Business, Form 8829: Expenses for Business Use of Your Home, Form 4562: Depreciation and Amortization, Schedule SE: Self-Employment Tax, Form 1040 ES: Estimated Tax,** and all forms related to hiring assistants.

Receipt Book for Child Care Services: A receipt book to be used for regular parent payments or to establish a record of yearly payments for both parent and provider tax returns. Each book contains fifty carbonless sets of receipts.

See page 138 for a further description of books available from Redleaf Press.

INTRODUCTION: CHILD CARE AS A BUSINESS

Family child care can be both difficult and rewarding. Few give as much of themselves or accept as great a responsibility as the family child care provider. Few are more deserving of the satisfaction that comes from helping the community's children learn and grow.

As a provider, you know those difficulties and rewards well. But there are others of equal importance to which you may not have given as much thought: making money . . . paying bills . . . paying taxes . . . dealing with governmental agencies and parents.

Taking care of children is only half your job. The other half is taking care of business.

It is in your best interest to know as much about taking care of business as you do about taking care of children. Parents will appreciate and expect it. The IRS demands it.

Family child care providers are considered self-employed taxpayers who must report their business income and expenses on the IRS form **Schedule C: Profit or Loss From Business**. Those who are paid to care for children but do not meet or are exempt from local child care regulations should also fill out a **Schedule C** each year. I encourage all providers to meet their local standards and file a tax return. As this book points out, however, even nonregulated providers can deduct many of the same business expenses as regulated providers.

I recognize that trying to follow all of the advice in this book at one time is a significant challenge for anyone. Don't try to read this book from cover to cover. Use it as your guide when you are looking for answers to specific questions about what is deductible and how to keep accurate records. Take your time. Ask for help when you don't understand something. Try to improve your business skills a little more each year. If you do so, your success is assured.

CHAPTER 1: BASIC RECORD KEEPING PRINCIPLES

There are good reasons for keeping complete, accurate, and ongoing records:

- You are in business to earn money. Good financial records tell you at a glance how you're doing. Without them, you may not know.
- Parents are entitled to, and will probably ask for, an account of payments made to you for their own income tax purposes.
- The Internal Revenue Service considers you a self-employed businessperson selling the service of child care. Other than a very few exceptions, *you must file a federal income tax return.* Good records help you figure the correct amount of tax you owe – no more, no less. They decrease the likelihood of problems with the IRS.

Keeping good records is not as difficult as it may sound. Essentially, all you have to do is keep track of the money that comes into, and the money that goes out of, your business. More specifically, you have to record your child care income and your business expenses as you incur them. Your net income (or profit), the money you've worked long and hard to earn, is the amount left after you've subtracted your business expenses from your income. It is also the amount that Uncle Sam will want to tax.

Because the information you need to record is so closely tied to taxes, the presentation of record keeping methods in this book is built around the tax forms. The *Basic Guide* attempts to simplify and make understandable the necessary information; it does not in all cases cover every possible detail. You may need additional sources of information from the IRS or a competent tax preparer if your family child care income and expense situation is unusual or complex.

The *Basic Guide* shows how to record income, expenses, attendance, and other necessary information using a *Calendar-Keeper* and various IRS publications. The *Calendar-Keeper*, designed as a wall calendar, is useful for keeping all of your records in one place. It includes space to record attendance and payment for each child, miscellaneous income, deductible business expenses, capital expenditures, and mileage.

The record keeping procedures shown here may be adapted for use in an ordinary spiral notebook as well. Just draw lines to make columns, and label the columns as shown in the *Calendar-Keeper* examples. You will also need envelopes for storing receipts. You may want to purchase a pocket calculator or other record keeping tools. The cost of an item used in keeping business records is a fully deductible business expense.

Here are some key principles of good record keeping:

1) It cannot be stressed too strongly that you need complete, accurate, and ongoing records. This includes records of parent payments, Child and Adult Care Food Program reimbursements, and all business expenses. Don't skip a week here and there; don't lose track of a receipt or two. You need to develop the habit of saving receipts and discipline yourself to update your records on a regular basis.

2) You are required to save your business records and receipts for three years from the date you file your tax return. It is probably a good idea to hold them for several additional years. Records of purchases that you are depreciating (house, home improvements, and other capital expenditures) should be kept for the life of the depreciation, plus three years.

3) Keep your business records as separate as possible from your personal records. One way to do this is to open up a separate business checking account. This is not required, but it may make it easier to track your family child care income and expenses. Deposit all your family child care income into this account and, from this account, pay for as many of your business expenses as possible. Some providers also have business credit cards separate from their family credit cards. In addition, a few items may have to be paid for with cash. Keep receipts for these expenses, total the amount each month, and write a check for that amount from your business account to your family account.

When you need money for family expenses, make out a check to your family checking account and record it as a "transfer of income," not as an expense. (This is how you pay yourself for doing family child care.) Try not to pay for family expenses directly out of your business checking account. Remember, a separate checking account can help you sort out your income and expense at tax time, but it's not an adequate substitute for good record keeping.

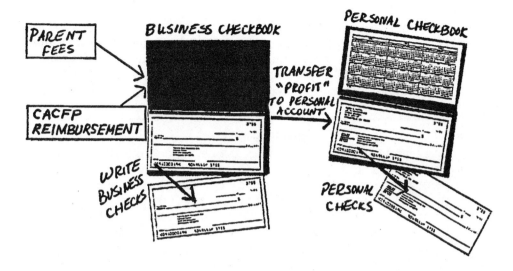

4) Make sure your receipts clearly show what you purchased. If not, mark the receipt to identify your business expenses. For example: If a receipt from a hardware store simply says "merchandise," write "mop," "plastic bucket," etc. next to the cost of each business item. Here are two receipts that illustrate this point.

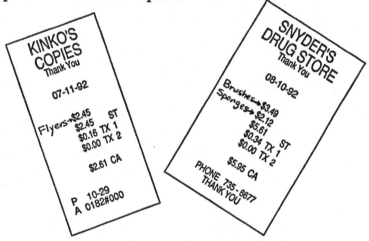

5) The IRS allows you to support your claim for business deductions with "adequate records" or by other "sufficient evidence" that does not have to be written. It is not necessary that you record every business activity at the time it was conducted. You have a great deal of leeway to reconstruct your records later on. For example: You don't have to record your business mileage each time you take a trip. You can

reconstruct your business trips at the end of the month or year by using receipts, bank deposit slips, field-trip permission forms, etc. Obviously, you are more likely to remember your business activities if you keep current with your record keeping. But you should not shy away from reconstructing records at a later date if you have to.

BARTERING

Some providers and parents occasionally do child care for each other. This can also happen between two providers. One person will care for the children on one day in exchange for the other person taking the children another day. No money changes hands. This is commonly called bartering. What are the tax consequences of bartering? Technically, when one party provides services to another party in exchange for something, a taxable transaction has occurred. Both parties must report the value of the service they receive as income, even if no money was exchanged. How do you determine the value of the services exchanged? You would probably look to what you normally charge for such care.

Let's say you and another provider exchange child care services of one day each and the value of each service is $20. You would each report receiving $20 as income from the other person. If the child care was given in order to care for children other than your own, you each can report the $20 you "spent" as a business expense. The net result would be no taxable income. If you provided $35 in services and received $55 in services, you would have as taxable income $20. If the child care was given by the other person to care for your own child in order to enable you to work, you may claim the value of services given towards your own child care tax credit. (See **Form 2441: Child and Dependent Care Expenses** for more details.)

You do not have to report as income any services you are receiving that are given to you without any expectation that something will be offered in return. This is not considered a bartering arrangement.

6) Although you may try to save every receipt from every business expense, what if you are missing some at the end of the year? Here are a few ways to piece together your records and back up your claim:

a) Save your canceled checks. They are not as good as receipts because they don't prove you bought a particular item, but they are better than nothing.

b) Save your credit-card statements. They may remind you of additional expenses or help you in your reconstruction. They are also evidence of expenses.

c) If you have no records of a field trip or a special outing with the children, ask the parents to write you a letter confirming that the event occurred.

d) Take photographs of items you purchased without receipts.

e) If you forget to obtain an occasional receipt (for instance, at a garage sale), write out your own receipt as soon as possible after the purchase. Put on the receipt a description of the item, the address where the item was purchased, date purchased, whom it was purchased from, how much it cost, and the method of payment (cash, check or credit card). Several such "receipts" written by you throughout the year and added to your files is probably acceptable. Writing 100 such receipts on April 14 is not. A sample reconstructed receipt is at left.

Customer's Order No.			Date 5/18 1992		
Name	Garage sale - Mrs. Allison				
Address	125 Portland Ave.				
SOLD BY	CASH	C.O.D.	CHARGE	ON ACCT MDSE. RETD. PAID OUT	
QUAN.	DESCRIPTION			PRICE	AMOUNT
	blue wooden high chair				
				$10	00
	pd cash				

ALL claims and returned goods MUST be accompanied by this bill.

Rec'd by

Early Childhood Education Center
Concordia University
7400 Augusta
River Forest, IL 60305
94-68

17

f) If audited, you can also testify yourself (or bring in other witnesses) to explain what happened. Don't give up in an argument with the IRS simply because you don't have every receipt. If you can make a good case for your position, you may succeed.

7) The appearance of your records can sometimes be as important as the records themselves. Try to keep your records in a clear, well organized fashion. It is easier to do this if you spend a little time at it each week. Many providers conduct a monthly review of their records to make sure everything is in order. At the end of each month, ask yourself these questions:

a) Have I recorded all parent payments?
b) Do I have complete attendance records?
c) Have I recorded all the hours I used my home for my business? (See Chapter 3.)
d) Have I kept a record of my business trips on my calendar or notebook?
e) Have I saved all my business receipts?
f) Do my receipts clearly identify what I bought? (If not, list what the item is on the receipt.)

Store your receipts and records by the expense category, not by month. If you are audited, the IRS will want to examine all expenses in a category (i.e. food), rather than examine all of your expenses for June or July. Put each category of records together into a folder or envelope and label it. At the end of the year it will be relatively easy to add up the expenses from each category.

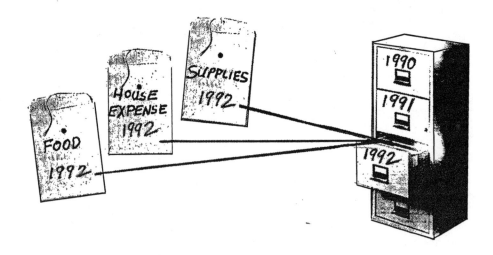

8) Mark your bank deposit slips to indicate the source of the deposit (i.e. child care business). The IRS may assume that any undocumented deposits are business income, and they may require you to pay taxes at your business rate on this amount.

Your goal is to have receipts for every penny of income and expenses associated with your business. It is not hopeless if you don't have every receipt. The more documentation and verbal explanation you can produce to justify your claim, the better chance the IRS will accept it.

Question: Should I operate under a business name?

Many providers use a business name ("Dee's Day Care," "Tender Care for Kids," etc.) and use it on their checks, advertising, parent contracts, etc. Although not a requirement, a business name can help you set a professional tone with parents and the IRS. It can also help you with keeping track of your business expenses. Consult your county clerk office about any local regulations for filing your business name.

CHAPTER 2: KEEPING TRACK OF INCOME, TAX CREDITS, AND PRE-TAX PLANS

Income is all the money you receive in exchange for providing child care. It includes payments:

- from parents (This includes gifts or bonuses received in the form of either money or gift certificates. Gifts of food or merchandise of nominal value are not considered income.);
- from the Child and Adult Care Food Program;
- from your state Human Services Department or other government or private agency that pays you to care for children;
- for family child care-related services you provide (e.g., conducting a workshop for other providers); and
- grants from the state or from local organizations for the purchase of equipment, home improvements, or other business items.

Your major source of income will be payments from parents for the care of their children. Since you may have some parents who pay hourly, some who pay based on part-time daily rate, and others based on a full-time flat rate, it is imperative that you keep accurate attendance and payment records for each child. Parents will also need this information for their tax records.

RECORDING INCOME

You can keep track of attendance and payments several ways, but you should always record 1) the name of the child being cared for, 2) the date of each payment, 3) the period of time covered by the payment, 4) the amount paid and the check number (if paid by check) or receipt number (if paid with cash). One method is to use a notebook and record when you receive payments. For example:

	January			
	4th - 8th	11th - 15th	18th - 22nd	25th - 29th
Louisa	$80 ✓#4286	$80 ✓#4310		
Terri	$80 ✓#6912	$80 ✓#7021		
Michael	$40 cash	$40 ✓#1675		

You may also consider using the *Calendar-Keeper* record keeping system

APRIL ATTENDANCE AND PAYMENT LOG   (To record drop-off and pick-up times that vary, try using two lines per child; or consider the larger calendar with 30 lines.)

CHILD'S NAME	S M T W T F S (1 2 3)	TOTAL	S M T W T F S (4 5 6 7 8 9 10)	TOTAL	S M T W T F S (11 12 13 14 15 16 17)	TOTAL	S M T W T F S (18 19 20 21 22 23 24)	TOTAL	S M T W T F S (25 26 27 28 29 30)	TOTAL	TOTAL
ROBERT	√√√√√	70	√√√√√√	70	√√√√√	70	√√√√√	70			280
JEFF	√√√√√	70	√√√√√√	70	√√√√√	70	√√√√√√	70			280
LISA	√ √ √	30	√ √ √ √	30	√ √ √	30	√ √ √	30			120
MICKY			√√	30	√√	30					60

WEEKLY TOTALS: 200 | 200 | 170 | 170 | | 740

FOOD PROGRAM TALLY

TOTAL # OF EACH MEAL SERVED		
BREAKFASTS	54	
LUNCHES	42	
SNACKS	54	
SUPPERS	—	
DATE CLAIM SENT 4/31	RECEIVED 4/20 (Mar)	

	CACFP INCOME REC'D	OTHER INCOME REC'D	PARENT FEE INCOME REC'D			
APRIL INCOME	99.61	25		=	APRIL TOTAL	765
BALANCE FORWARD	318.27			=	BALANCE FWD TOTAL	2275
TOTAL Y-T-D INCOME BY CATEGORY	417.88			=	TOTAL Y-T-D	3060

© Copyright 1992 Redleaf Press

Whether you use the *Calendar-Keeper* record keeping system or a notebook, be sure to keep a monthly total of all income, plus a year-to-date total. This will help you avoid errors caused by adding long columns of figures. You will want to add the total amount paid by parents to all other day care income received to get your total monthly income. Record your yearly income (arrived at from your monthly totals) on Part I of **Schedule C**. See the *Family Child Care Tax Workbook* for details on recording income on **Schedule C**.

Most providers use what is called the "cash accounting method" of record keeping. This means that you record the income when you receive it and record the expense when you pay it. In other words, if a parent pays you in January for care you provided in December, you report the income for the January year. But if you receive a check from a parent in December that you don't cash until January, you count it as December income. If you make a credit card purchase in December but don't pay the bill until January, it's a December expense. It's considered an expense at the time you make the charge. If a parent walks out without paying, you simply don't report the money they owe as income.

It is good business practice to get paid in advance for the child care you are providing. Most child care centers make parents pay at the beginning of the week or month. You should do the same. It protects you from parents who don't pay on time–or at all. It also helps set the proper business tone for your relationship with the parents you serve. If a parent can't pay everything in advance, ask her to pay an increasing amount at the beginning of each week until she reaches the full payment. For example: You charge $80 a week and regularly collect fees on Fridays. If you want to start collecting fees on Monday, have parents pay you $10 on Monday and $70 on Friday for the first week. For the second week, have parents pay $20 on Monday and $60 on Friday. Continue this until all $80 is being paid on Monday.

Some providers try to avoid paying taxes by not reporting their income. They ask parents to pay in cash and to not claim the child care tax credit for their children. In turn, the provider often agrees to charge the parents less for taking care of the children. Providers who do not report their income to the IRS should understand that they are breaking the law. If they are caught they will have to pay back taxes, interest, and perhaps penalties. Because they aren't reporting their income, many providers are not keeping receipts and records of business expenses. This means that, if caught by the IRS, they will have fewer expenses to claim and more taxes to pay.

In addition, providers should be aware that the parents may decide at the end of the year to claim the child care tax credit, despite their promises not to do so. The parent is always entitled to claim this credit, regardless of any previous agreement with the provider. If this happens, the provider is likely to be audited. Readers of this book will understand that there are hundreds of business deductions they can claim to reduce their taxes. I hope that all providers will report their income, claim their allowable deductions and encourage others to do so.

CHILD AND ADULT CARE FOOD PROGRAM

The United States Department of Agriculture Child and Adult Care Food Program (CACFP) helps providers serve nutritious meals without passing on the rising costs of groceries directly to the parents. It is part of the same federal program that reimburses schools and day care centers for providing nutritious meals.

There has been a lot of confusion within the IRS regarding whether or not providers should report CACFP reimbursements as income. IRS publications have given out contradictory advice over the years. Recent IRS investigations into this subject may help clarify this issue. Watch the latest edition of the *Family Child Care Tax Workbook* for the most correct information. Until the IRS issues something definitive, my best advice is that if you receive money from the Child and Adult Care Food Program, you should report it as income. You may put this amount on the line "Other Income," or on the line "Gross Receipts or Sales" on Part I of your **Schedule C.**

If your Food Program sponsor gives you a **Form 1099** that indicates how much in reimbursement you have received during the past year, it is critically important for you to indicate on your **Schedule C** that you are reporting this reimbursement as income. Enter the amount on the line "Other Income" and mark "1099 income" on the line so the IRS will know that you are declaring this. The IRS is very likely to check your **Schedule C** to see if any **1099** income was reported.

Question: Why should I report my CACFP reimbursements as income? What's wrong with saying my food expenses are equal to my reimbursements and declaring these two numbers a "wash"?

There are several important points about CACFP reimbursements that all providers should understand. The IRS can always deny your food deductions if you don't have the proper receipts. If you are not showing any income or expenses for food on your tax form, the IRS may consider it likely that you do not save receipts and investigate. Also, some providers don't spend as much money on food for the children they care for as the Food Program reimburses them. They will have to pay tax on the overpayment. The IRS could audit you and demand to see all of your receipts before they will allow you to write off any of the Food Program reimbursements.

A more important reason not to treat your food expenses as equal to your Food Program reimbursements is that you will probably be cheating yourself! In more than ten years of training thousands of providers across the country, I have found that the vast majority of providers spend more on food than they receive from the Food Program. This happens for many reasons: Providers are serving some foods that are not eligible for reimbursement; providers serve a snack or meal that is not covered by the Food Program; providers care for children that occasionally eat more than the usual amount; or providers buy and serve some special, more expensive food on occasion. The Food Program reimbursements were never intended by the USDA to cover all the food expenses of a provider.

24

Some IRS agents tell providers that they cannot claim any food expenses that exceed the reimbursement amount. This is not correct. You are entitled to deduct all ordinary and necessary business food expenses, regardless of your reimbursement total. By keeping close track of these expenses, you are more likely to claim a higher deduction. (See page 78 for a complete explanation of how to keep good records of food expenses.)

Question: How do I treat the income I receive from the Food Program for my own child?

Some providers receive Food Program reimbursement for their own children because their families are low-income. The IRS does not consider this reimbursement as income for a provider's family. Providers can handle this situation in one of two ways. Let's say you received $2,500 from the Food Program one year, and $500 of this amount represented reimbursement for your own child. Your food expenses for the year (not counting the food served to your own child) was $2,700. Your first choice is to report only $2,000 as income on **Schedule C** and list $2,700 as food expenses. Your second choice is to report $2,500 as income and list $3,200 as food expenses ($2,700 + $500).The result of using either method is the same: You will pay no tax on reimbursements for your own children.

Question: My husband says I shouldn't join the Food Program because we will pay more in taxes. Is this true?

He's right, but he's also wrong. Yes, you will pay more in taxes, but the reason for this is that you will have more income and therefore more profit at the end of the year. Ask yourself this question, "Would I like to win the lottery?" Of course you would. Your answer would still be "yes" even knowing that you would have to pay taxes on your winnings because you would end up with more money at the end of the year. Joining the Food Program operates the same way. You are going to spend virtually the same amount on food whether you are on the Food Program or not, so getting reimbursed for the cost of this food means money in your pocket. Paying taxes on this new money just reduces the amount you get, but you always will end up richer. Let's look at an example to see how this works:

Monthly Income	Before Joining CACFP	After Joining CACFP
Parent fees ($75 a week X 4 weeks X 4 children)	$1200	$1200
CACFP income (we'll use an average of $55 a month per child) 4 X $55 = $220	0	$220
TOTAL MONTHLY INCOME	$1200	$1420
Monthly Expenses		
Food (food expenses may be higher with CACFP)	$250	$250
Other (regular monthly expenses such as household supplies, car mileage, plus a portion of ongoing expenses such as depreciation of furniture and appliances; toys; property tax; utilities; insurance; interest; publications; etc.)	$500	$500
TOTAL MONTHLY EXPENSES	$750	$750
Taxable income (total income minus total expenses)	$450	$670
Taxable yearly income (net monthly income X 12 months)	$5400	$8040

(You must pay self-employment tax and income tax on your taxable income. Tax rates may change from year to year, but we will use the 1992 rates of 15.3% for self-employment tax [on 92.35% of taxable income] and 28% for an income tax rate. Even if these rates change, the principle illustrated by this example will remain the same.)

	Before	After
Self-employment tax	-$763.00	-$1136.02
Income tax	-$1512.00	-$2251.20
PROFIT ON YOUR BUSINESS	$3,125.00	$4,652.78

By joining the CACFP, the provider has raised the taxable income from $5,400 to $8,040 a year. More important, the profit rose from $3,125.00 to $4,652.78 a year; an increase of $1,527.78. Yes, more taxes were paid, but profit is a lot higher, and that is what is most important.

Note: Some providers do not want to join the Food Program because they worry that they will be pushed into a higher tax bracket and they will end up with less profit. This is not true. If you are pushed into a higher tax bracket because of reporting the Food Program reimbursement as income, it just means that your Food Program income is taxed at a higher rate. The rest of your income remains taxed at the lower rate. You still will benefit by being on the Food Program.

FORM W-10 AND THE CHILD CARE TAX CREDIT

Providers should be careful to properly record their parent income for several reasons. The IRS wants to know how much you made, and you can run into trouble if the parents of the children you care for don't accurately report their child care expenses.

Many parents are eligible for a child care tax credit on their federal, and sometimes state, tax returns. This credit is based on family income and how much a parent pays for child care. To claim this credit, a parent needs to obtain his or her provider's social security number or taxpayer identification number. To get this information, parents will ask you to fill out **Form W-10:Dependent Care Provider's Identification and Certification.** It is the parents' responsibility to give this form to you. If a parent doesn't ask you to fill out this form, you do not have to do anything. If the parents have left you earlier in the year and you have not heard from them since, you do not need to track them down. Providers face a penalty of $50 for not giving out their correct number to a parent or for refusing to fill out **Form W-10.** Even providers who do not file tax returns or do not meet local regulations must give out their number when presented with **Form W-10.** To make things run smoothly with parents, many providers take the initiative by filling out **Form W-10** and presenting it to parents before being asked to do so.

It won't do any good to try to hide your income from the IRS by refusing to sign **Form W-10.** The parent will simply indicate on his or her child care tax credit form that you refused to give your number. This, by itself, will probably trigger an IRS audit of you. If a parent asks you for your social security number over the telephone, you should say that you prefer to fill out the **Form W-10.** You are not required to give your number verbally. If a parent who left owes you money and is now asking for your number, you may want to say you'll do so only when she or he pays up. You could stall filling out

Form W-10 for this parent until April. If you do not want to use your social security number with parents, you can get your own taxpayer identification number from the IRS. Ask for **Form SS-4: Application for Employer Identification Number** and fill it out. You will receive your identification number in the mail or over the phone if you call.

The IRS has started to use computers to compare how much parents are claiming to spend on child care with how much providers are reporting as income. The **Form W-10** does not ask you to report how much the parent paid you, so you do not know what parents are reporting on their forms. If the numbers don't match, there is a strong likelihood that you will be audited. The most important thing you must do is keep accurate records of how much each parent paid you for the year.

There are circumstances in which parents may be tempted to cheat. They may not be able to track down one of the providers they used and decide to put down all their payments under your number; they may put down more than they paid you by mistake; or they may simply want to cheat.

How can you protect yourself from a parent who reports spending more on child care than you received? The best way is to give each parent a receipt at the end of the year. The receipt should have on it the name of the child, the amount paid for the entire year, the months covered by the payment, the date the receipt was signed, your signature, and most importantly, the parent's signature. Keep a copy of the signed receipt and give the parent a copy. Without the parent's signature, the parent could argue later that the amount is incorrect. If the parent refuses to sign the receipt, mark on it that the parent refused to sign and save it. Any one of the three forms below can be used as a receipt: the **Form W-10**, a sales book purchased from a drug store or a receipt book sold by Redleaf Press.

$2500 in child care to Diane Provider in 1992
Polly Parent

Form W-10
(Rev. August 1990)
Department of the Treasury
Internal Revenue Service

Dependent Care Provider's Identification and Certification
(Do NOT file with your tax return. Keep for your records.)

Part I Dependent Care Provider's Identification (See instructions)

Name of dependent care provider
Diane Provider

Provider's taxpayer identification number
123-45-6789

Address (number and street)
123 Baldwin Street

If the above number is a social security number, check this box ▶ . . . . [X]

City, state, and ZIP code
St. Paul, MN 55104

Certification and Signature of Dependent Care Provider.—Under penalties of perjury, I, as the dependent care provider, certify that my name, address, and taxpayer identification number, as shown above, are correct.

Please Sign Here

Signature of Dependent Care Provider
Diane Provider

Date
1-1-92

Part II Name of Taxpayer Requesting Part I Information (See instructions)

Name, street address, city, state, and ZIP code of person(s) requesting information

Polly Parent 456 Target Lane St. Paul, MN 55115

No. _89_   _3-19_   19 _92_

Received from _JOHN AND MADELYNE CRAWFORD_ $ _$85 00_
                        (parent/guardian name)

EIGHTY-FIVE DOLLARS AND NO/100 _____ Dollars

☐ Cash
☒ Check # _2430_   For Child Care Services from _3-19-92_ to _3-23-92_
                                        M D Y   M D Y

Provider's Signature _Ann Thomas_

Parent's Signature _Madelyne Crawford_

Customer's
Order No.   Date _1 / 1_   1992

Name _Mrs. Albertson_

Address

SOLD BY	CASH	C.O.D.	CHARGE	ON ACCT.	MDSE. RETD.	PAID OUT

QUAN.	DESCRIPTION	PRICE	AMOUNT
	For child care		
	services for		
	Jenny Albertson		
	1/1/92 - 1/8/92		
	_pd._	8 75	00
	Mrs. Albertson		
	Mrs. Sidner		

ALL claims and returned goods MUST be accompanied by this bill.
Rec'd by

Having signed receipts makes it unlikely that parents will claim a different amount on their child care tax credit forms. If a parent does, that parent will have to explain why the amount on their form is different from the amount shown on your signed receipt. You can help keep parents honest by explaining that they are likely to be audited if the amount they claim for their child care tax credit does not equal the amount on your receipt.

PRE-TAX CHILD CARE BENEFIT PLANS

Another area in which providers should be working closely with parents for mutual advantage is pre-tax child care benefit plans. Increasingly, employers are offering a benefit plan that allows employees to designate some of their wages to pay for child care expenses before these wages are subject to any taxes. Parents who don't spend all of the money they set aside under this plan each year must return any unspent money to their employer. By participating in such plans, parents lower their taxable income and pay less in taxes. Employers also benefit by paying less in social security taxes on the lower taxable income. Such plans are given various names: flexible benefit plan, cafeteria plan, salary reduction plan, or pre-tax spending account.

94-68

Let's look at an example of how such plans work:

Jane is married, has one child, and in 1991 paid $3,000 in child care
expenses, earned $30,000, and filed a joint tax return:

	No Pre-Tax Plan	Pre-Tax Plan
Calculation of Taxable Income		
Adjusted Gross Income	$30,000	$30,000
Salary Reductions for Child Care	$0	- $3,000
W-2 GROSS WAGES	$30,000	$27,000
Standard Deduction	- $5,700	- $5,700
Exemptions	- $6,450	- $6,450
TAXABLE INCOME	$17,850	$14,850
Calculation of Federal Taxes		
W-2 Gross Wages	$30,000	$27,000
Federal Income Tax	$2,681	$2,231
FICA Tax (7.65%)	$2,295	$2,066
TOTAL TAXES	$4,976	$4,297
Child Care Expense	$3,000 (after tax)	$3,000 (before tax)
NET INCOME (after taxes and child care expenses)	$22,024	$22,703

By setting aside $3,000 before taxes for child care expenses, Jane has saved
$679 in federal taxes. Her employer saved $229 in lower social security and
Medicare employment taxes.

Note: The numbers in this example will likely be different after 1991 because
of changing tax rules, but the principle will remain the same.

How can providers benefit from flexible benefit plans? Providers should ask
parents if they work for employers that offer such plans. If a parent does, you
should strongly encourage him or her to participate. Use the chart on this
page to illustrate how the parent can save money. In addition, you could ask
the parent to review the materials given out at work that describe the benefits
of the plan. You should not be shy about suggesting that parents might pay
you more once they are participating in such plans. They will be paying lower
taxes and have more take-home pay available for higher child care costs.
(Tell parents that you are going to raise your rates but it won't effectively cost
them anything more.)

If the parents are participating in flexible benefit plans, they will ask you to sign receipts for child care payments on a regular basis. Be careful not to sign any receipts that say you've received payment for your services, if you have not received the money. Ask parents to pay first, then sign the receipts. It is a different situation if a receipt is serving as a bill that a parent must submit to an employer before payment can be released. Signing such statements is proper. The reason for caution here is to avoid the situation where you've signed a form stating that you've received some money and then the parent leaves without paying you. The IRS will assume you were paid the money and they will expect you to report it as income.

POTENTIAL BONUS OPPORTUNITY

You may be able to get a bonus from your parents that won't cost them anything. Here's how. Find out how much money each parent has set aside in his or her child care fund account. Ask when the plan ends each year (usually it will be at the end of the calendar year). A couple of months before the end of the year, estimate whether the parent will spend all the money in the fund. Parents who don't spend all the money in their funds will lose it; the money must be returned to the employers, according to federal law. Since parents will lose it unless they spend it, ask that any remaining amount be paid to you.

For example, a parent set aside $3,000 for child care, but you estimate he will only spend $2,800 by the end of the year. Ask for the unspent $200 as an extra payment to you. (You must report this as taxable income. I recommend that you don't agree to kickback some of this bonus to a parent, because you must declare the entire amount as income and pay taxes on it.) Parents may wish to prepay this unspent money for the next year, but the law prevents them from doing this, so don't allow them to use leftover plan money to prepay you.

CHILD CARE TAX CREDIT FOR YOUR OWN CHILD

Ordinarily, providers may not take advantage of the federal child care tax credit because they are caring for their own children. But if you pay another caregiver to care for your own child, you are eligible to claim your expenses towards the child care tax credit on your personal tax return. Some providers send their own children to a nursery school or a preschool because of a special program or because the children will get more attention there. In addition, if you hire a caregiver to care for your child while you are attending a provider training workshop, you can also claim this expense towards your child care credit. This is because you are "at work" while taking training that is related to your business. Providers must meet the same rules as other parents to qualify for this credit. The cost of sending your child to an overnight camp does not qualify for the tax credit. See **Form 2441: Child and Dependent Care Expenses** and **Instructions for Form 2441** for further information.

The IRS Tax Code says that parents who use child care programs operated for the "well-being" of children are eligible to claim their expenses towards the tax credit. Child care programs that are operated for the "education" of children are not eligible. This law was written long before the rise in professionalism and the growing consensus in the child care field that there is little difference between "child care" and "education." In practice, the IRS considers programs for children below the first grade not to be "educational" and thus eligible for the tax credit. Eventually, the Internal Revenue Code may have to be amended to avoid any confusion as to which child care programs count for tax credit. What is clear is that providers can claim this credit if they are paying for child care for their own children, in the same way that other parents do.

MILITARY HOUSING ALLOWANCES

There are a number of providers across the country whose spouses work for the U.S. military. The military gives housing allowances to its personnel based on rank and geographic location. A typical allowance is approximately

$500 per month. These housing allowances are not taxable income to the military family. Are there any tax consequences to the military family that is operating a family child care program?

1) If the provider's family is living on a military base

The military has its own set of licensing standards that providers must meet before they can operate family child care homes. These standards supersede local and state rules or regulations. For providers who live on base, their housing allowances are applied towards their living quarters. The provider's family pays nothing for housing except for telephone costs. The provider cannot claim as a business expense any house expenses such as rent, utilities, insurance, repairs, depreciation, property tax, and the interest on the mortgage.

2) If the provider's family is not living on a military base

The provider does not have to meet any military licensing standards and falls under the local/state regulations. Whether the provider's family rents or owns a house, the housing allowance is not taxable income and does not need to be spent entirely on housing costs.

A provider who is buying a home may *always* deduct the Time-Space percentage of property tax and mortgage interest as a business expense if the provider meets or is exempt from local licensing/registration regulations. The remaining amount may be claimed on **Schedule A,** if the provider itemizes. If the housing allowance is enough to cover all the costs of buying a house, the provider may not take a business deduction on any other housing costs (utilities, insurance, etc.). If the allowance does not cover all these costs, then the provider's family can deduct a portion of the out-of-pocket costs using this formula:

Total family − Housing ÷ Total family X Out-of-pocket X Time/ = Business
income   allowance income   housing costs   Space% deductible
                                                       expense

Let's illustrate this with an example: A provider earns $10,000 and her spouse earns $20,000 from the military. Their housing allowance is $6,000. Their housing costs total $7,000 and are broken down as follows: property tax $3,000, mortgage interest $1,000, utilities $1,500, house depreciation $500 and house insurance $1,000. Their Time-Space percentage is 30%. This provider can claim $900 of her property taxes ($3,000 X 30% T-S%) and

$300 of her mortgage interest ($1,000 X 30% T-S%) as a business expense. Because her housing costs exceed her housing allowance by $1,000, she can also claim a portion of this as a business expense:

Total family income	−	Housing allowance	÷	Total family income	X	Out-of-pocket business expense	X	Time-Space%	=	Business deductible expense

$20,000
$10,000
 $6,000
$36,000 − $6,000 = $30,000 + $36,000 = 83% X $1,000 = $830 X 30% = $249

If the provider's family is renting and not buying a home, the provider is not incurring any mortgage interest or property tax costs and therefore may not claim any business deductions for these. If the housing allowance covers all the housing expenses (i.e., rent), the provider may not claim any housing expenses as business deductions. If the allowance is not enough to cover housing expenses, the provider may deduct a portion of her out-of-pocket expenses using the same formula as described above.

Providers who have additional questions about how to treat housing allowances and deduct housing expenses should consult with a representative from the military, the IRS, or ask a tax professional. See also Internal Revenue Code section 265 and **Publication 17,** Chapter 6.

Running a family child care business is not as simple as it may first appear. But if you are aware of the rules of the CACFP, child care tax credits, and pre-tax benefit plans, you will be better able to protect yourself against IRS audits and maximize your profit.

CHAPTER 3: TIME-SPACE PERCENTAGE

The Time-Space percentage is the most important number to calculate for your business. This number represents the portion of your home that is used for business purposes. You will use this number to determine how many of your expenses that are used for both business and personal purposes can be deducted as business expenses. These expenses include:

Casualty losses
Mortgage interest
Real estate taxes
House insurance
House repairs and maintenance
Utilities
House depreciation
Personal property depreciation
Major home improvements
Land improvements
Household supplies and toys

Because these costs are substantial, calculating your Time-Space percentage correctly is very important. The higher your Time-Space percentage, the greater your business deductions.

The Time-Space percentage is calculated using the following formula:

$$\frac{\text{Number of hours your home is used in business in a year}}{\text{Total number of hours in a year}} \; X \; \frac{\text{Number of square feet of your home that are used for business}}{\text{Total number of square feet in home}} = \text{Time-Space percentage}$$

To compute your Time-Space percentage use a three step process.

STEP ONE: CALCULATE YOUR TIME PERCENTAGE

How much time is your home used in your business? The formula for computing your Time percentage is:

$$\frac{\text{Number of hours your home is used in business in a year}}{\text{Total number of hours in a year}} = \text{Time percentage}$$

The following activities may be counted in calculating how many hours you are using your home for your business:

- Caring for children
- Cleaning the home for your business
- Cooking for children in your care
- Planning and preparing activities for your business
- Keeping business records, including meal planning and preparing shopping lists
- Preparing paperwork for the Child and Adult Care Food Program
- Conducting interviews with prospective parents
- Talking to parents and other providers on the telephone about your business
- Any other activities that you spend time on in your home that are for business purposes

An important note: You may not count time that you spend out of the home on activities such as shopping or transporting children to school. In these two examples, you are not using your home for business purposes.

Many providers are not including all of their business hours in the calculation of their Time percentages and thus are not taking full advantage of the law. It is very important to keep track of these hours so that you can back up your claim. Below is a further description of how to record these business hours.

WORKING HOURS WHEN CHILDREN ARE PRESENT

Throughout the year you should maintain records that indicate how much time you spend caring for children. Keep regular attendance records or save a copy of something that identifies your normal working hours (for example, a parent contract or a flyer advertising your business). If you don't have anything in writing that identifies your regular hours, ask parents to sign a statement that lists your hours. Such a statement can be very simple:

"My child, Karla Haley, was cared for by family child care provider Maureen Bailey from February 1, 1992 to December 31, 1992. During that time my child was cared for on a regular basis from 7am to 5pm, Monday through Friday.

Signed: Mrs. Ariel Haley - January 15, 1993."

Let's say you cared for children from 7:00 a.m. to 5:00 p.m., five days a week: 10 hours a day X 5 days a week X 51 weeks = 2,550 hours. You may not double count any time and you cannot count more than 24 hours in a day. For example, on Monday you may not count ten hours caring for Julian plus another ten hours caring for Marsha, if the two children were present at the same time.

You should count the hours when the children are in your care, from the time the first child arrives to when the last child leaves. If you usually work from 7:00 a.m. to 5:00 p.m. but a child occasionally arrives early or stays late, make sure you note this on a calendar or your record book and count this additional time. If the last parent arrives to pick up her child at 5:00 p.m. but stays to talk with you until 5:30 p.m., you should count the extra 30 minutes of work.

If a child stays overnight occasionally, count all the hours the child is in your house. If your normal hours are 7:00 a.m. to 5:00 p.m., but on some days the first child doesn't arrive until 7:15 or 7:30, you may be able to take an assertive position and count the hours beginning at 7:00 a.m. Why? Because you are ready to do business during your normal business hours. It is just like a gas station that opens its doors at 6:00 a.m., but the first customer doesn't arrive until 6:30 a.m. The gas station is ready to do business at 6:00 a.m. and all expenses incurred between 6:00 a.m. and 6:30 a.m. (salaries, utilities, etc.) are business expenses. As long as you keep regular hours, it is unlikely that the IRS will challenge about some children occasionally arriving late or leaving early.

You must be reasonable about calculating your regular business hours. If the first child never arrives before 8:00 a.m., you can't say you are open at 7:00 a.m. You can't claim you are open 16 hours a day just by saying you are available to care for children 16 hours a day. You must actually care for children on a regular basis during that time. If you offer child care 24 hours a day, I would only count those actual hours you care for children. You may be available to work 24 hours a day, but it is unreasonable in this situation to claim hours you aren't working. If you are paid by parents for holidays or vacation days, count these hours. If you want to take an assertive position, you could count the hours for occasional days you take off, but the IRS may not accept this position if they know you are doing this.

You must develop a system to keep track of the extra time, beyond your regular business hours, that you care for children. You may use a calendar to record these hours. For example:

JANUARY

S	M	T	W	T	F	S
DECEMBER '92 / FEBRUARY					1 NEW YEAR'S DAY	2
3	4 Sharon leaves 5.30	5	6 Todd arrives 6:45	7 Maria stays overnight 5 pm – 5 pm FIRE DRILL DAY	8	9
10	11	12	13	14	15	16

DECEMBER '92
S M T W T F S
1 2 3 4 5
6 7 8 9 10 11 12
13 14 15 16 17 18 19
20 21 22 23 24 25 26
27 28 29 30 31

FEBRUARY
S M T W T F S
1 2 3 4 5 6
7 8 9 10 11 12 13
14 15 16 17 18 19 20
21 22 23 24 25 26 27
28

You could also record these hours with your attendance records. For example:

JANUARY ATTENDANCE AND PAYMENT LOG

(To record drop-off and pick-up times that vary, try using two lines per child, or consider the larger calendar with 20 lines.)

CHILD'S NAME	S	M 1	T 2	W	T	F	S	TOTAL	S	M 3	T 4	W 5	T 6	F 7	S 8 9	TOTAL	S	M 10	T 11	W 12	T 13	F 14	S 15 16	TOTAL	...
Andre	8	8	8½	9	10			43½	8	8	8	8	8			40	8	8½	9	8	8			41½	
Philip	8	10	9	10	8½			45½	8½	9	8	8				41½	8½	9	9	8	8			42½	
Tanya	8	10	9	10	10			47	8	9	9	9	9			44	8	9	9	9	9½			44½	

If you care for children on an irregular basis, it will be necessary to do more paperwork to calculate the total number of hours you are caring for children in a year. Let's say you started your business with two part-time children. After two months you took on a full-time child. During the summer you worked 50 hours some weeks and 20 hours other weeks, depending upon parent vacations. In the fall you only cared for two school-age children a few hours each morning and afternoon. With this kind of schedule you would need to track your working hours each week and add up the total at the end of the year. Your different weekly schedules might look like this:

3	4 7am-9am 3pm-5pm	5 7am-9am	6 7am-9am 3pm-5pm	7 7am-9am FIRE DRILL DAY	8 7am-9am 3pm-5pm	9
10	11	12	13 3pm-5pm	14	15 3pm-5pm 4TH QTR 1988 ESTIMATED TAX DUE	16
17	18 7am-5pm MARTIN LUTHER KING JR. DAY	19 7am-5pm	20 7am-5pm	21 7am-5pm	22 7am-5pm	23
24 / 31	25 7am-3pm CALL YOUR LOCAL R&R AGENCY—UPDATE YOUR SERVICE	26 7am-5pm	27 7am-3pm	28 7am-5pm	29 7am-3pm	30

The main point to remember is that you must keep careful records that show how many hours you are caring for children over the entire year. The more working hours, beyond your regular hours that you can document, the higher your Time percentage will be.

WORKING HOURS WHEN CHILDREN ARE NOT PRESENT

In addition to counting all the hours you are caring for children, you may also include hours spent using your home for business purposes when children are not present. This includes time spent cleaning, cooking, activity planning (reading magazines to find recipes, cutting out pictures for a craft project, developing a lesson plan, etc.), record keeping, interviewing, phone calling, and other activities that are business related. Do not count hours spent away from home, even if you are conducting business activities such as shopping or transporting children to school. You must be in your home for you to claim that you are using your home for business purposes. Also, do not count hours spent in general house repair or maintenance activities (cutting the lawn, repairing fixtures, putting up storm windows, etc.).

You may not count these hours if you are also caring for children at the same time. For example, if you are cleaning the house during the day while the children sleep, you cannot count the cleaning hours because you are already counting this time while caring for children. You may only count these hours when children are not present.

You must keep records showing that you spent these hours on business activity and not on personal activity. If you spend one hour cleaning up after the children leave, count this hour as business time. If you are doing general house cleaning, count only that time that is associated with the mess created by your business. It is a good idea to record when you are doing personal cleaning because this makes your business records more believable. Mark on a calendar when you conduct a business activity or else prepare a weekly schedule that you regularly follow.

Some providers conduct their business activities (for example, cleaning, cooking, activity preparation and record keeping) on a scheduled basis. If this is true for you, prepare your weekly or monthly schedule and use the hours in your schedule as an average for the year. To support such a schedule, keep actual track of your hours for several different weeks throughout the year. This amount of record keeping should be sufficient, as long as you follow your schedule. Let's look at an example of a monthly schedule:

January

						No Hrs Open
						Other Hrs Worked
						Previous Total
						Y-to-Date Total

S	M	T	W	T	F	S
DECEMBER '92 / **FEBRUARY**					1 Clean 6:30–7am 5:30–6pm record keeping NEW YEAR'S DAY ½ hr	2 Prepare next week's activities 2 hrs
3 Personal cleaning 3 hrs Bake 1hr	4 Clean 6:30–7am 5:30–6pm	5	6	7 FIRE DRILL DAY	8 → record keeping 1 hr	9
10 Bake 1hr	11 Clean 6:30–7am 5:30–6pm	12	13	14	15 → record keeping 1 hr 4TH QTR 1992 ESTIMATED TAX DUE	16
17 Bake 1hr	18 Clean 6:30–7am 5:30–6pm MARTIN LUTHER KING JR DAY	19	20	21	22 → record keeping 1 hr	23
24 ↓ Bake 1hr 31	25 Clean 6:30–7am 5:30–6pm CALL YOUR LOCAL R&R AGENCY—UPDATE YOUR SERVICE	26	27	28	29 → record keeping 2 hrs	30 ↓

DECEMBER '92

S	M	T	W	T	F	S
		1	2	3	4	5
6	7	8	9	10	11	12
13	14	15	16	17	18	19
20	21	22	23	24	25	26
27	28	29	30	31		

FEBRUARY

S	M	T	W	T	F	S
	1	2	3	4	5	6
7	8	9	10	11	12	13
14	15	16	17	18	19	20
21	22	23	24	25	26	27
28						

BUSINESS TOTALS

Cleaning	22.0	hours
Cooking	4.0	hours
Activity preparation	8.0	hours
Record keeping	5.5	hours
TOTAL BUSINESS HOURS	39.5	hours

If you don't keep a regular schedule for your business activities, you should record your hours on a weekly basis on your calendar or in your notebook. Try to record these hours every week. If you can't remember to do this, try to keep careful records for several weeks during different parts of the year. If the hours you worked these weeks are typical of how much you work throughout the year, use the average of these weeks for your calculation. For example:

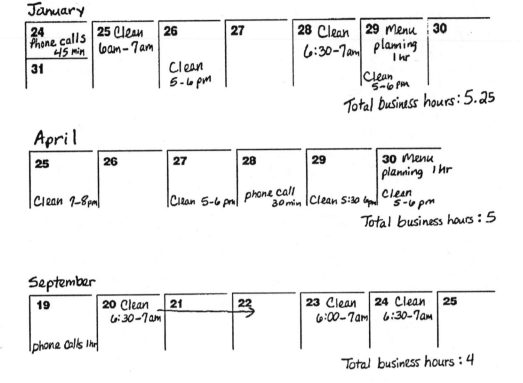

January

24 Phone calls 45 min	25 Clean 6am - 7am	26 Clean 5-6 PM	27	28 Clean 6:30-7am	29 Menu planning 1 hr Clean 5-6 PM	30
31						

Total business hours: 5.25

April

25 Clean 7-8pm	26	27 Clean 5-6 pm	28 phone call 30 min	29 Clean 5:30 6pm	30 Menu planning 1 hr Clean 5-6 pm

Total business hours: 5

September

19 phone calls 1hr	20 Clean 6:30-7am	21	22 ⟶	23 Clean 6:00-7am	24 Clean 6:30-7am	25

Total business hours: 4

Average number of business hours per week: 4.75

If these weeks are typical, add 242.25 hours (4.75 X 51 weeks) to your total of the hours you are caring for children during the year to determine your Time percentage.

Here is a summary of how to total your business hours to calculate your Time percentage:

Regular work hours 7:00 a.m. - 5:00 p.m.	
10 hours a day X 5 days a week X 52 weeks =	2,600 hours
Children occasionally staying late	
1 hour late X 2 times a week X 51 weeks =	102 hours
Children staying overnight	
14 hours (5pm - 7am) X 6 occasions =	84 hours
Provider takes a one-week vacation	
50 hours not in business that was counted above =	-50 hours
Cleaning up after children are gone	
1 hour a day X 5 days a week X 51 weeks =	255 hours
Cooking for the business	
1 hour on Sunday (baking) X 51 weeks =	51 hours
Planning activities	
1 hour on Saturdays X 51 weeks =	51 hours
Record keeping	
2 hours a week X 51 weeks =	102 hours
Parent interviews	
6 interviews X 2 hours each	12 hours
Talking to parents on the phone	
1 hour a week, on average X 51 weeks =	51 hours
TOTAL HOURS =	3,258

$$\frac{3,258}{8,760 \text{ (hours in a year)}} = 37\% \text{ Time percentage}$$

KEEPING TRACK OF EXTRA HOURS

Is it worth it to record all the extra hours caring for children, cleaning, preparing activities, and so on? Consider the example above. If this provider had only counted her regular work hours, her Time percentage would have been 30% (2,600 work hours divided by 8,760 total hours). Instead, when she included her additional work hours, it was 37%.

The additional hours counted in this example are not unusual. Many providers may have a larger number of work hours in their businesses. This difference of 7% can be significant. For every $1,000 of expenses that the Time-Space percentage is applied to (assuming the Space percentage is 100%), this provider's business deductions increase by $70. If there were $10,000 in such expenses, the provider increases her deductions by $700. Depending upon the provider's tax bracket, this could mean a savings of almost $300 in federal taxes each year.

A recent national survey of regulated family child care providers (*A Profile of Child Care Settings* by Mathematica Policy Research, Inc.) offers some insight into the life of an average provider:

- Providers offer care an average of 55 hours per week
- 25% of providers offer care 60 or more hours per week
- 74% of providers operate 50 or more weeks per year
- 13% of providers offer evening-hour care
- Approximately one-third of providers plan children's activities, spending an average of 3 hours per week on planning.

Although this survey was based on scientific sampling methods, the results should only be used as general background information. Your work schedule may vary considerably from these averages. If necessary, you might want to use this data to help you educate your tax preparer or the IRS about the long hours that providers work.

THE IRS POSITION ON HOW TO CALCULATE THE TIME PERCENTAGE

Many tax preparers and some IRS agents have said to providers that they can only include the hours they are caring for children in their Time percentage calculations. This is not true, and providers can point to three authoritative sources that support the explanation of the Time percentage offered in this chapter.

In January 1992, the IRS issued Revenue Ruling 92-3, the most complete description of the Time-Space percentage the agency has ever published. (See Appendix A for a copy of the complete Ruling.) The Ruling defines the Time percentage as "...the total hours in the year that the day care business is operated (including substantiated preparation and clean-up time), divided by the total number of hours in a year." In the example in the Ruling, the provider spent one-half hour before and one-half hour after regular business hours preparing for and cleaning up after the children. These hours were included in the Time percentage.

The second source of authority is a 1990 Tax Court decision. In this case, the court allowed a provider to claim additional hours spent in preparation and cleaning in calculating business time. See: *Robert B. Neilson and Dorothy F. Neilson v. Commissioner*, CCH Dec. 46,301; Dkt. 4014-88, January 2, 1990, 94 Tax Court No. 1. (A portion of this case is reproduced in Appendix B.)

44

The third authority is a letter written in 1990 by an IRS official to former Minnesota Senator Rudy Boschwitz: "Hours spent cooking, cleaning and preparing activities for the business could be included in the calculation of the time-space percentage... If a child care provider spends one-half hour setting up for the children and one-half hour returning a room to personal use, in addition to seven hours actually in the presence of the children, a provider could claim that eight hours were expended in the trade or business of providing day care for children."

With these three sources of authority, you should insist upon your right to claim these hours in the calculation of your Time percentage.

Question: What if I began doing child care in the middle of the year?

Count those hours you were using your home for your business and divide by the total number of hours in the weeks you were in business. Apply your Time-Space percentage only to those shared business and personal expenses that you paid during the months you were open for business. For example: If you were in business August to December and you worked an average of eleven hours per day, five days a week, your Time percentage would be 33% (1,210 [22 weeks X 55 hours of work per week] divided by 3,696 [22 weeks X 168 total hours in a week]). You would calculate your Space percentage the same way, as if you had been in business for the entire year (see description below for how to calculate the Space percentage). If your utility bills were $500 for August to December and your Time-Space percentage was 33%, you would claim $165 as a business expense ($500 X 33%). For yearly expenses such as house insurance, property tax, etc., you would claim your Time-Space percentage of these expenses, adjusted for the months you were in business. For example: If your house insurance was $800 a year and your Time-Space percentage from August to December was 35%, you would claim $116.67 as a business expense ($800 X 5/12 of the year X 35%).

Question: I haven't kept careful records of how many hours I used my home for my business. What should I do now?

Start tracking your business hours today. If you are in the middle of a year, start recording business hours for the next few months. If your average for these months is typical of what you worked earlier in the year, use these average weekly hours for the entire year.

You can also use today's records to help you reconstruct records for an earlier year. Let's say it is January of 1993. You are doing your taxes for 1992 and you realize that you didn't keep track of all of your business hours for 1992. You should take several weeks in January and record your actual business hours (caring for children, cleaning, preparing activities, etc.). Maybe your numbers show you worked an average of 60 hours a week during three weeks in January. If these three weeks are typical of what you did in 1992, use 60 hours a week as an average for your Time percentage calculation for 1992. Continue recording your business hours for the rest of 1993 to help you calculate your Time percentage for 1993. If the three weeks of record keeping in January are not typical of what you worked in 1992, you must come up with some other reconstruction of records to show what your work pattern was like in 1992.

A final comment about the Time percentage: the more hours you are claiming to be working for your business, the more complete your records should be. It is not necessary to write down your business hours on a calendar or in a notebook every day of the year. You should have records for at least several weeks during different times of the year. Having several months of complete records is even better. If you are audited, the IRS is likely to look at your records to see if they are reasonable and question you to see if you are believable. Proving that you worked an extra three hours a day for your business may be extremely difficult without adequate records. The IRS may decide to give you one extra hour a day but no more. Your records and your ability to come across as believable are all you have on your side to persuade the IRS to allow you to claim those additional two hours a day. If you have good records, you should claim everything you are entitled to.

In reading this so far you may decide that it is too much work for you to do all this record keeping. You don't have to claim these extra hours of work when children are not present if you don't want to. Getting started on a record keeping system, even one that you feel comfortable with, is difficult. Maybe it will take another year before you begin tracking all your hours properly. It is never too late to start.

STEP TWO: CALCULATE YOUR SPACE PERCENTAGE

The formula for computing your Space percentage is:

$$\frac{\text{Number of square feet of your home that are used for business}}{\text{Total number of square feet in your home}} = \text{Space percentage}$$

When can you count space in your home as being in business use? According to the 1992 IRS Revenue Ruling 92-3 (See Appendix A for a copy of the complete Ruling), business space is defined as space "...that is available for day care use throughout each business day and that is regularly so used in that business." A room does not have to be used every business day for it to be considered regularly used for business. But a room that is ordinarily restricted from child care use and used occasionally for the business is not considered regularly used for business.

Let's look at several examples:

1) A provider's bedroom is used two hours a day for naps by the children. Regular business use? Yes.
2) A child's bedroom that is only used when the children are sick. This happens three times a month. Regular business use? No.
3) A study room on the second floor that contains a provider's desk and file cabinet where she does record keeping and menu planning five hours a week. Regular business use? Yes. (This study room could be counted as business use even if local regulations prohibited children in care from being on the second floor.)
4) A laundry room that is used four hours a week for business cleaning (sheets, pillow cases, towels, children's clothes, etc.) and ten hours a week for personal cleaning. Regular business use? Yes.
5) A storage room that contains 25% business and 75% personal items. Regular business use? Yes.
6) A garage that stores a car, bicycles, and outdoor toys that are used in the business. Regular business use? Yes.
7) A basement area that the provider's husband uses for his hobby workshop. Regular business use? No.

WHAT COUNTS AS SPACE

A provider should look at each room in his home and ask this question: Is the space available for business throughout each business day and is it regularly used by my business? If the answer is "yes," count all the space in the room as business use. If the answer is "no," do not count any of the space as business use. Most providers regularly use the kitchen, living room, dining room, bathrooms, entryway, hallways, playroom, most storage rooms, most bedrooms, furnace area (the business uses heat, hot water and air conditioning), and laundry room for their business. Include closets as part of individual rooms.

Do not include in the total square feet of the home any space that is unusable (an unfinished attic or unfinished basement). Also do not include the lawn area, driveway, garden or patio as either a business or personal part of the home. Do include as part of the home a porch, attached deck, or garage. You may also include as part of the home an unattached garage or other structures on your land such as a shed or greenhouse. (See IRS **Publication 587: Business Use of Your Home**, for support for this position.) A practical note: Many providers and their tax preparers don't include the garage, porch or attached deck in the total square feet of their home. The IRS has not paid much attention to this issue. If you don't use these areas for your business, you would be better off not to count them as part of your home at all. If you do use them for your business, you may want to include these areas.

Once you have looked at each room and determined whether or not it is used regularly for your business, add up the square footage in those business rooms and divide by the total number of square feet in the home. You might want to draw a simple diagram of the floor plan of your home, showing the square footage of each room. Here is an example:

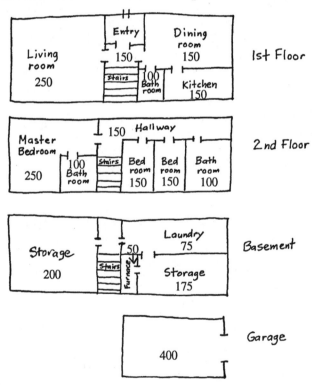

Let's add the square feet in our example:

	Used regularly for business	Square feet to count as business space	Square feet to not count as business space
Living room	Yes	250	
Dining room	Yes	150	
Kitchen	Yes	150	
Bathroom	Yes	100	
Entry way/stairs	Yes	150	
Second floor hallway/stairs	Yes	150	
Master bedroom/bath	Yes	250	
Child's bedroom	No		150
Child's bedroom	No		150
Bathroom	Yes	100	
Basement laundry room	Yes	75	
Basement furnace area	Yes	50	
Basement storage area	Yes/No	175	200
Detached garage	Yes	400	
TOTAL		2,000	500

$$\frac{2{,}000 \text{ square feet used for business}}{2{,}500 \text{ total square feet of home}} = 80\% \text{ Space percentage}$$

Many providers regularly use all the rooms in their homes for business and thus their Space percentage would be 100%. If this is the case for you, you need not measure the square feet of every room in your home. Instead, estimate the total square feet of your home and use this number as business square feet as well.

STEP THREE: CALCULATE YOUR TIME-SPACE PERCENTAGE

Now multiply the Time percentage by the Space percentage to get your Time-Space Percentage. Using our example:

37% Time X 80% Space = 30% Time-Space percentage

You must recalculate your Time-Space percentage every year. It will vary slightly from year to year. There is no limit to how high your Time-Space percentage may be (up to 100%). The vast majority of providers are claiming a percentage of between 25% and 40%. If you have the records to support your claim, you should not hesitate to put whatever percentage you have calculated on your tax return. Use **Form 8829: Expenses for Business Use of Your Home** to report your Time-Space percentage.

Question: I use a playroom in my home exclusively for my business. How do I take this into account in calculating my Time-Space percentage?

The IRS is only concerned with whether you are using a room on a regular basis for your business. It doesn't matter if the room is used two hours or twenty-four hours a day for business. In either case all the space will be counted as business use. A provider who uses all of his rooms regularly will have a higher Space percentage than one who uses a few rooms exclusively for business and has other rooms that are not used regularly for business. A provider who has a room that is used only for business does have one advantage because he may deduct 100% of the cost of the items in this room as a business expense. (See Chapter 5 for a discussion of how to claim household expenses.)

Question: Do I have to use my Time-Space percentage on all my expenses that have both business and personal uses?

No. The Time-Space percentage is a reasonably accurate formula for allocating expenses between business and personal uses. For some items the percentage may be too low in measuring business use, for other items it may be too high. But for most providers it is a fair measure overall. A majority of providers will find it simplest to use their Time-Space percentage on all shared expenses. (Note: Do not use the Time-Space percentage on food expenses.)

You are not required, however, to use the Time-Space percentage for all your shared expenses. There may be some expenses that are used much more in your business, such as paper towels, toilet paper, toys, or other items. If this is the case, you may want to calculate an actual business-use percent to determine how much of the cost to deduct for your business.

Let's say you are using 80% of the paper towels you buy in a year for your business. If so, you could deduct 80% of this total cost as a business expense. This would give you a higher deduction than by using your 30% Time-Space percentage. If you are calculating an actual business use instead of using your Time-Space percentage, you must have some record to show how you came up with the higher percentage. Mark your receipt with your estimated business use percent, or make a note of how often you are using the item for business and personal purposes.

A note of caution: using an actual business-use percent for smaller items or for several large items is proper. Be careful, however, not to claim an actual business-use percent on every item that is used more than your Time-Space percentage amount and then use your Time-Space percentage on all other items. If you do this you are undermining the general purpose of the Time-Space percentage and the IRS could ask you to use an actual business use for every item.

Question: I do child care in a building separate from my home. How does the time-space percentage affect me?

An increasing number of providers are using separate buildings to run their child care business. Make sure you check with local regulations to see if this is allowed. If you use a separate building for only your day care business, you may deduct 100% of the costs associated with this building (rent, utilities, insurance, phone, maintenance, etc.) as a business expense. You wouldn't use a time-space percentage for this building. If it's used only for child care, it would be 100%.

Note: You cannot count any of the distance driving between your home and your separate building as business mileage. This is considered commuting. You can count business trips to and from your business site or business trips to and from your home to other businesses as business mileage.

CHAPTER 4: DIRECT BUSINESS EXPENSES

You are entitled to take a business deduction for all the expenses that are "ordinary and necessary" costs of operating your family child care business. What is an ordinary and necessary expense may depend upon the facts and circumstances of a particular situation and could vary from one provider to another. Obviously, you want to take every deduction to which you are legally entitled. Doing so will reduce your taxable income to the smallest possible figure. To claim all of your allowable deductions, you need to keep complete, accurate and ongoing records of all your business expenses. This chapter and the next will identify all the typical family child care expenses.

TYPES OF BUSINESS EXPENSES

There are three types of family child care business expenses:

I. Direct business expenses: Items that are purchased for use by the business and are generally used up within one year. Providers must take these as business deductions all in one year. Such expenses include (in the order they appear on **Schedule C**):

    Advertising
    Bad debts
    Car expenses
    Employee benefit programs
    Insurance (besides house insurance)
    Interest (besides mortgage interest)
    Legal and professional services
    Office expenses (bank charges, books, magazines, dues, etc.)
    Rent of business property (besides an apartment)
    Repairs and maintenance of personal property
    Supplies
    Taxes and licenses (besides real estate taxes)
    Travel, meals, and entertainment
    Telephone
    Wages
    Other Expenses
        Food
        Household items
        Yard supplies

II. House expenses: Items that are purchased to maintain your home. Providers may take a portion of the cost of these expenses (your Time-Space percentage) as business deductions in one year. Such expenses include:

> Casualty losses
> Mortgage loan interest
> Real estate taxes
> House insurance
> House repairs and maintenance
> Utilities
> House rent

I will discuss house expenses in detail in Chapter 5.

III. Capital expenditures: Expenses that are related to the purchase of your home or the improvement of the value of your home, your land, and your personal property. Providers may take a portion of the cost of these expenses (your Time-Space percentage) as business deductions, but the expense must be spread over a number of years by using depreciation rules. Such expenses include:

> House
> Major home improvements
> Land improvements
> Personal property
> Automobile

I will discuss capital expenditures in detail in Chapter 6.

Question: What deductions may I take if I am not licensed?

If you are paid to care for children and you do not meet your local/state regulation requirements, you may still deduct many expenses as business deductions as long as you report your income. These deductions include all the direct business expenses listed in this chapter as well as personal property depreciation explained in Chapter 6. The only expenses you would not be entitled to deduct are the following house expenses:

> *Mortgage loan interest*
> *Real estate taxes*
> *House insurance*
> *House repairs and maintenance*
> *Utilities*
> *House rent*
> *Casualty losses*

House depreciation
Major home improvements
Land improvements

Many illegal providers try to avoid reporting their income to the IRS because they are concerned about paying taxes. I don't recommend that anyone ignore local/state regulations, but if you are operating illegally, you should be aware that you can still claim a large number of business deductions.

An important note: Providers who are exempt from their local regulations are entitled to claim all the same deductions as a licensed or regulated provider. Example: If state law only regulates those providers who care for four or more children, a provider caring for less than four children would be exempt from regulations and could claim the same business deductions as a regulated provider. If your state or local government does not have any child care regulations, you are considered legal and may claim all business deductions.

Question: When may I start claiming business deductions?

Let's look at two examples.

Example 1: A provider starts caring for two children in January. Her state regulations say that providers caring for more than four children must be licensed. In July the provider applies for a license and starts caring for six children. In November the provider receives her license. IRS **Publication 587: Business Use of Your Home** states that you can begin deducting house expenses if you "have applied for, been granted, or been exempt from having a license, certification, registration, or approval... as a family or group day-care home under applicable state law. You do not meet this requirement if your application was rejected or your license or other authorization was revoked." In our example, the provider should be reporting all parent fees as income. In January the provider can start claiming all house expenses because she is exempt from licensing. In July she can continue to claim these expenses because she has applied for a license, even though she is now in violation of local regulations. She can claim all direct business expenses for the entire year whether or not she meets local regulations.

Example 2: A provider begins caring for six children in February. Local regulations require a license if providers care for more than four children. In October she applies for a license and she receives it in January of the following year. In this situation the provider could not start claiming house expenses until she applied for the license in October. She should claim all direct business expenses and report all income starting in February.

A general comment about deducting business expenses: There are very few instances in the Internal Revenue Code or in IRS publications when family child care is identified by name. The rules for determining which deductions may be claimed as business expenses are generally the same for every business. Often the regulations are not clear and you must decide how the rule should be interpreted. I encourage you to apply a common-sense approach to the rules and use a standard of "reasonableness" to support your views.

Throughout this chapter we will come across situations that are gray areas, where the regulations are vague. I will suggest two different solutions to each situation: a conservative and an assertive interpretation. The conservative position is one that is extremely unlikely to be challenged by the IRS and will result in a relatively lower business deduction. The assertive position results in a relatively higher business deduction, but it is more likely to be challenged by the IRS.

When I describe an assertive position in this book, I believe that many providers (although not necessarily all) can make a reasonable argument for this position based on their own situation. You may have to argue with the IRS to win this position, and I cannot predict how the IRS will rule. Winning or losing usually depends upon the particular facts and circumstances in each case and the individual auditor's opinion.

CALCULATING DIRECT BUSINESS EXPENSES

Direct business expenses should be deducted in one year if they are used up within one year. Examples of such items are car expenses, insurance, interest, rent, repairs, taxes, wages, and food. Some items such as large toys, small appliances, and tools, may last longer than a year. The Internal Revenue Code says that items lasting longer than one year must be taken as an expense over a number of years, using depreciation rules. See Chapter 6 for a description of depreciation. As a practical matter, however, the IRS has a rough rule of thumb that allows taxpayers to deduct the item in one year if it costs less than $100. This means that if you buy a $50 highchair for your business, most IRS auditors will let you claim all of this expense in one year.

How much of the cost of the items listed in this chapter can be deducted as business expenses? The answer depends on how the item is used. Any item you purchase will fall into one of three categories: 100% business use, 100% personal use, or shared business and personal use.

If the item is used exclusively for your business, you may claim 100% of the cost as a business expense. Exclusive business use means just that. If you buy a pocket calculator to do your business records and use it even once for personal purposes, you can't claim it as a 100% business expense. You may, however, claim that a puzzle is a 100% business expense even if your own children play with it during the time the children you care for are present. If your children play with the puzzle after the other children are gone, the puzzle is no longer just a business expense.

If the item is used exclusively for personal use, you may not claim any of this expense for your business. Personal grooming supplies, jewelry, novels, antiques, and eyeglasses are examples of purely personal expenses.

Last are those expenses used partly by your business and partly for personal purposes. Many of these expenses are household items such as cleaning supplies, kitchen utensils, and small toys. The simplest way to allocate such shared expenses is to apply your Time-Space percentage to the cost and claim the result as a business expense. If you wish, you could also determine an actual business-use percent for these shared items and deduct the business portion. If you use this method, you should keep some type of record to show how you determined the actual business-use percent. It probably only makes sense to use an actual business-use percent for items that have a very heavy business use.

Let's look at how to treat expenses in the three basic categories:

	100% Business	100% Personal	Time-Space (30%) Shared	Actual Business Use % Expense	Business Deduction
Fee for workshop	$15.00				$15.00
Wages for assistants	$250.00				$250.00
Crayons	$7.25				$7.25
Jewelry		$45.00			0
Light bulbs			$5.60 (X 30%)		$1.68
Yard hose			$18.50 (X 30%)		$5.55
Paper towels				$32.00 (X 75%)	$24.00

This example shows how important it is to recognize what type of expense you have in order to know how much of it can be claimed as a business expense.

Itemized in the following section is a comprehensive, but not complete, list of direct business expenses for family child care providers. I have lumped these expenses together as you might want to record them in your *Calendar-Keeper record keeping system* and on your **Schedule C**. The expense categories on **Schedule C** change over the years, so the categories listed below may not match exactly. A few of the expense categories on **Schedule C** do not apply to family child care and you should leave these lines blank (example: commissions and fees). You can make your own decision about how to group your expenses. You will never be penalized for putting an expense under one of the categories listed below instead of another. I recommend that you do not lump the majority of your expenses into just one category such as "supplies." This could trigger an IRS audit because it may appear to be an unusually high single expense for your business. Use the several blank lines at the end of the listing of expense categories on **Schedule C** to enter some of your expenses. I recommend that you list food, household items, and yard supplies here separately.

Not every provider will be able to deduct all the expenses listed. Each expense must be used for your child care business for it to be deductible. For instance: Two providers have gardens. The first provider has the children care for the plants in her garden as part of their weekly activities. This provider could therefore deduct at least part of such expenses as garden gloves, wheelbarrow, and plants, because they are being used in her business. The second provider does not permit the children to work in her garden. As a result, none of the expenses would be a business expense for her.

START-UP EXPENSES FOR YOUR BUSINESS

If you are just starting out to do family child care, when does your business begin: At the time you begin buying supplies? When you advertise for your first child? When you begin caring for children? When you get a license? Your business begins from the time you are ready to accept your first child in care. You don't have to be caring for children or have a license, or even meet local regulations before the IRS will consider you in the business of doing child care. All expenses you incur after you are ready to care for children (advertising, supplies, etc.) can be deducted in the same way that you would deduct expenses after you begin enrolling children.

New providers should note that there is a difference in how to treat expenses incurred after you begin your business and start-up expenses incurred before your business begins. Start-up expenses are those expenses incurred after you have decided to do family child care and before you are ready to accept your first child. These expenses could include a first-aid kit, advertising, travel, books, crib, supplies, etc. Such expenses cannot be deducted in one year as they could if they were purchased after the business had started. These expenses must be treated as capital expenses and amortized (the cost spread evenly over sixty months).

For example, if you started your business in April, and you bought $30 worth of small toys strictly for your business in May, you could deduct $30 in your first year of doing business. If, however, you purchased the items in March, as start-up costs, you cannot deduct them all in the first year. See the *Family Child Care Tax Workbook* for further details on how much of start-up expenses may be claimed in the first year.

TYPICAL DIRECT BUSINESS EXPENSES

ADVERTISING

You can deduct the cost of newspaper ads; T-shirts; radio ads; buttons; a rubber stamp with your business name and return address for mailing letters; tote bags; bumper stickers; yard, magnetic, and window signs; business cards; balloons; an answering service; flyers; a Yellow Pages listing; membership dues to your local Chamber of Commerce or other business organization; and other forms of business advertising.

BAD DEBTS

Some providers believe that if a parent leaves owing them money, they have a bad debt loss. Not so. The only time a provider can claim a bad-debt loss is when the parent pays by check in one year, the provider reports this money as income on her tax return, and the check bounces the next year. This is unlikely to happen. When parents leave owing money, providers should simply not report this owed money as income. There is therefore less income to pay taxes on.

CAR EXPENSES

There are two methods to choose from in calculating expenses associated with driving your automobile for business purposes:

1) Use the standard mileage rate method, or
2) The actual automobile expenses method.

Most providers will probably use the standard mileage rate to record automobile expenses. If you bought a new automobile recently and drive it a lot in your business, it may be more beneficial to claim a percentage of actual expenses. You may want to figure your automobile expenses using both methods and then use the method that gives you higher deductions.

Providers should check to see if they are covered by insurance when using their car for their business. If you are not, purchase the proper insurance, even if it is not deductible, or check with each child's parent to see if the parent's car insurance covers the child when travelling with you.

METHOD 1: STANDARD MILEAGE RATE
The standard mileage rate varies each year (1992 rate: 28 cents per mile); check the *Family Child Care Tax Workbook* for the current-year rate. The rate is intended to cover most car expenses, including gas, repairs, and insurance.

You need to keep "sufficient written evidence" (IRS language) of how many miles you drove your automobile for your business. You do not have to keep a log in your car and record odometer readings every time you drive. Here is a convenient way to keep records of your business miles:

Step One: Begin marking on your calendar or a notebook the destination of each business trip and the day you took the trip. For example:

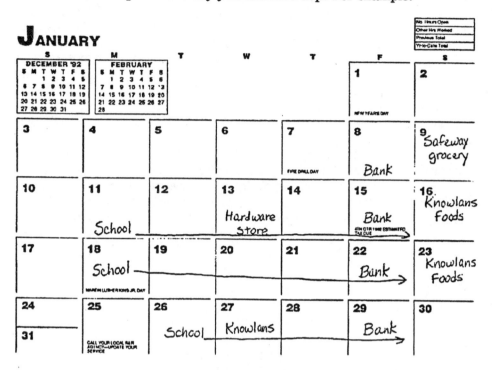

At the end of the year, go back through your calendar and prepare a list of all the destinations and how many times you traveled to each one. If you haven't marked your calendar, go through your records to uncover "sufficient written evidence" of business trips. These records may include receipts, canceled checks, bank deposit slips, field trip permission forms, entrance tickets, and photographs. Ask the children if they remember any trips you took them on. If so, get their parents to write you a note that says their child took a trip with you. Try to review your records monthly to make sure you don't forget a trip. If necessary, you could reconstruct all of your trips at the end of the year. (Note: It is always better to record your mileage trips as close as possible to the time you take them. Try to review your records at least monthly to keep up-to-date.)

Step Two: Drive from your house to the first destination you list and record the distance to that location. Repeat this for each destination.

Step Three: Multiply the mileage to and from each destination by the number of trips to each destination you took that year. Add the miles together for all the destinations and multiply by the standard mileage rate. The total is your business mileage deduction for the year. In addition, you may claim expenses for parking fees, tolls, bus, subway, taxi and train fares. You may also claim a portion of your state and local personal property taxes on your car and a portion of any car loan interest, according to the percent of miles you drove your car for your business. For example: if you drove your car 45% of the time for your business, you could deduct 45% of your car loan interest payments. See the *Family Child Care Tax Workbook* for more details.

You may not claim the costs of business car insurance or repairs to your car that were caused by driving it for your business. To deduct these expenses you must use the second method of claiming car expenses described below. *This is true even if you purchase a special insurance policy or rider to cover your business use of the car.* If you drive more than one car in your business at different times, you may claim the standard mileage rate for the business miles you drove with each car.

Example:

Al's Grocery Store	26 trips X 3 miles = 78 miles
First Bank	12 trips X 2 miles = 24 miles
Como Park	12 trips X 5 miles = 60 miles
Tots Toy Store	10 trips X 4 miles = 40 miles
Safeway Grocery Store	26 trips X 2 miles = 52 miles
Other trips (list)	1746 miles
TOTAL	2000 miles

2000 miles X 28 cents (1992 rate) = $560.00

Once you have measured the mileage to and from each destination, you can use this mileage number forever.

If you take a trip for both business and personal reasons, you may still deduct the entire mileage as a business expense if the trip is "primarily" for business purposes. The hardest trip to judge is one where you drive to the grocery store and buy groceries for both business and personal use. There is no hard rule about whether you can deduct the mileage for such a trip. If the trip was "primarily" to buy groceries for business, then you can deduct it as a business trip. Factors that might make it more clearly a business trip expense are: 1) You purchased more groceries for business than personal use; 2) You made other, separate, personal trips to the grocery and this trip was for regular business shopping; and 3) You took some of the children along with you to the grocery store (call it a field trip). Never try to claim every trip to the grocery store as a business trip, even if you always buy more business food than personal food. The IRS will say that there must be some personal trips for food.

You must list your business and personal miles driven in your car on **Form 4562: Depreciation & Amortization** when you file your tax return. Make a note at the beginning and end of each year of your odometer reading so you will know how many total miles you drove your car. Enter your car expenses on the line "Car and Truck Expenses" **Schedule C.** Make a copy of your records showing how you calculated this amount and put it into a file for next year's tax records so you won't have to remeasure the distance to the places you traveled.

METHOD 2: ACTUAL AUTOMOBILE EXPENSES
To use this method, first calculate the percentage of miles you drove your car for your business. Do this by dividing the number of business miles you drove in the year by the total number of miles you drove your car. Multiply the result by 100. For example: If you drove your car 10,000 miles in a year, and 2,000 of these miles were for your business, then your business use is 20% (2,000 ÷ 10,000 = .20 X 100 = 20%).

Write down on a separate piece of paper your actual car expenses for the year for gasoline, oil, tires, repairs, insurance, taxes, car lease payments, interest on the automobile loan, license, garage rent, car wash, lube, battery, anti-freeze, etc. (You may not deduct the cost of parking or speeding tickets, even if they were received on a business trip.) Make sure that you keep accurate records that document these expenses. In our example this total is $1,650.00. Multiply this result by your business-use percent and add any expenses that were 100% business. In the following example, the total is $630.00.

Gasoline	$575.00	
Oil	20.00	
Repairs	205.00	
Insurance	500.00	
Taxes & license	100.00	
Car loan interest	250.00	
	$1,650.00 X 20%	= $330.00
additional child care car insurance	$300.00(100%)	$300.00
Total		$630.00

Method 2 also allows you to take a depreciation deduction on your automobile. You would be able to claim part of the cost of the car (its fair market value at the time you began using it for your business) spread over a number of years. For example: if your car was worth $6,000 when you began using it for child care and your business use was 20%, you could claim $1,200 as a business expense over several years using depreciation rules. See the *Family Child Care Tax Workbook* for current rules on how to depreciate your car.

You may decide to use the standard mileage rate method one year and then switch to the actual automobile expenses method the next year. Once you start using the second method, however, you cannot switch back to the standard mileage rate unless you used the straight line depreciation method for the car. Most providers use the standard mileage rate to claim expenses for their car because it requires less record keeping. But Method 2 will probably show a higher business expense if you have a newer car and drive many miles for your business.

EMPLOYEE BENEFIT PROGRAM
Providers who hire assistants for their business do not have to pay them any benefits beyond the wages paid. If you do offer benefits such as health and dental care, retirement plans, etc., you may claim 100% of these expenses.

INSURANCE
You can deduct 100% of the cost of any family child care liability and accident insurance policy. (See Chapter 5 for a discussion of homeowner's and renter's insurance.)

You may deduct the business portion of any insurance you carry on your personal property (furniture, appliances, etc.) using your Time-Space percentage. (For car insurance rules, see section on Car Expenses on page 63.) The cost of car insurance is not deductible unless you use the actual automobile expenses method of claiming car expenses.

The cost of any life insurance policy is not deductible. While the cost of disability insurance is not a deductible expense for a self-employed person, I recommend purchasing it. Disability insurance pays you for your lost income if you become disabled and cannot work. Providers can easily become disabled enough not to be able to care for children. According to national studies, nearly one out of every two people ages 25 to 40 will become disabled for 90 days or more before they reach age 65. If your child care business is your sole source of income, or if your family relies on this income, you should seriously consider purchasing disability insurance to protect yourself. You may buy either short-term (up to six months) and/or long-term (after six months) coverage.

Rules regarding the deductibility of health insurance premiums for you, your children, and your spouse have changed often in recent years. Consult the *Family Child Care Tax Workbook* for the latest information.

SOME EXPENSES THAT ARE NOT ALLOWED AS BUSINESS DEDUCTIONS

According to the Internal Revenue Code, some expenses are never considered as business deductions. For instance:

Charitable contributions: Deduct as personal itemized deductions.

Disability insurance.

Life insurance.

Personal clothing: Only clothes that you wear that are *not* suitable as regular apparel when you are away from child care may be deducted as business expenses. Sweatshirts or T-shirts displaying a family child care design that you wear are not deductible. Clothing that would be deductible (i.e., not personal) includes items such as special storytime aprons or clown outfits. Clothing that you loan to children (mittens, caps, coats, etc.) is deductible. Clothing that you give to children may be deducted as a gift (business deduction limit of $25 per child per year). If you give children clothing such as T-shirts bearing your business name, they may be deducted as an advertising expense rather than as a gift if the children wear it outside where the public can see it. Children's clothing that parents give to you should be considered a gift, not income.

Pet care: The normal costs associated with a dog, cat, or other family pet (food, license, dog house, cat scratching post, and immunizations) are not deductible. You may deduct the cost of immunizations only if they are not required of all pet owners according to your local laws. The cost of a pet muzzle is deductible if it is necessary to protect the children.

INTEREST

You may deduct the full cost of interest charged on items purchased for 100% business use. For example, if you purchase a swing set for $700 on your credit card and pay $50 in interest for this item during the year, and if you used the swing set only in your business, you may deduct the full $50. If your own children also used the swing set, you may deduct the Time-Space percentage (for example: $50 X 25% = $12.50). If you can show that the swing set was used more than your Time-Space percentage, you may claim a higher percent of the interest. For example: $50 X 80% business use = $40.

Recent tax changes eliminated the deductibility of personal interest for taxpayers who itemize their returns, but self-employed taxpayers, such as family child care providers, can continue to deduct the full amount of interest associated with business purchases. (See the section on House Expenses on page 92 for a discussion of home mortgage loan interest.)

LEGAL AND PROFESSIONAL SERVICES

According to 1992 IRS Ruling 92-29, tax preparation fees to file your business tax forms are deductible as a business expense. The cost of preparing personal tax forms may only be deducted on **Schedule A.** Professional assistance for your business, such as accounting, legal services, and bookkeeping services is also deductible as a business expense. If someone does your personal and business taxes, have her bill you separately for each service. Legal fees and court costs for suing a parent in small claims court for not paying are also deductible.

OFFICE EXPENSES

Below are examples of business expenses to include under the category of office expenses.

Bank charges: Deduct all costs associated with keeping a separate business checking account. You may also deduct a portion of the costs of a personal checking account if you write some business checks from it. Deduct the portion of your personal checking account costs based upon the percentage of checks that are written for your business. For example, if 10% of the checks you write are for your business, deduct 10% of the cost of the checks as a business expense. If a parent bounces a check and the bank charges you a $12 fee, get the parent to reimburse you. If you can't reclaim this expense from the parent, you can deduct it as a business expense.

Books: *Basic Guide to Family Child Care Record Keeping, Family Child Care Tax Workbook, Calendar-Keeper: A Record Keeping System for*

Child Care Providers, and other tax publications or child care related books (first-aid and medical emergency books, for example) are all 100% deductible. Books such as an encyclopedia are only partially deductible if you have young children of your own. Deduct this expense based on the percent use of the books by your business.

Birthday/Christmas/holiday/get well cards for the parents or their children

Bulletin board

Business forms (field trip permission, medical information, registration, infant schedule, accident report, etc.)

Calendar
Chalkboard

Computer software, disks, paper, printer ribbons, and other supplies. (Deduct the portion of the cost of these items according to the percentage of time you used your computer for your business.)

Dues: The cost of local child care association dues and membership fees in organizations such as the National Association for the Education of Young Children and the National Family Day Care Association are fully deductible.

Education/Training: You may deduct the full cost of classes, workshops, and other training activities for your business, except for those education expenses necessary to obtain a license or to meet any initial regulation requirements in your state. If your licensing rules require you to take a certain number of hours of training in the first year of your license, all of your expenses for this training are deductible. Education expenses can be deducted for anything that is reasonably related to your child care business such as classes in child development, taxes and record keeping, CPR, parent communications, and nutrition. You may be able to deduct the cost of an educational class for tax purposes, even if you can't get credit for such classes to meet local regulation requirements.

Envelopes
Ledger

Magazines: You may deduct the cost of magazines that you use for your business. These may include children's magazines such as *Sesame Street, Scholastic, Ranger Rick's Nature Magazine, Jack and Jill, Highlights for Children, Totline,* and *Turtle Magazine for Preschool Kids.* Provider magazines may include *Family Day Caring Magazine, Parents, Working Mother, Good Housekeeping, Family Circle, Redbook,*

Better Homes and Gardens, Women's Day, American Baby, Pre-K Today, National Geographic, World, Parenting, Consumer Reports, Sunset, and Child.

If you have young children of your own, or if you normally buy some of the magazines listed above, the IRS may claim that these magazines are personal expenses. A provider using the conservative approach would only deduct those magazines that were purchased and used exclusively for her business. A provider using the assertive approach would deduct those magazines that contain recipes or business-related articles on child development, children's activities, and small-business advice. If you purchased the magazines primarily for your business, deduct the full cost.

Notebook/notepads
Paper, computer paper
Parent contracts
Pencils, pens, pencil sharpener
Photocopying costs
Pocket calculator
Postage stamps
Provider newsletter
Receipt books
TDD (Telecommunication Device for the Deaf) phone to receive calls from deaf parents

RENT OF BUSINESS PROPERTY

You may deduct the cost of renting items for your business such as VCR movies, Nintendo and other computer games, carpet cleaning machine, party equipment, etc. If your own children use these games or movies after the other children have left, deduct your Time-Space percentage of the rental fee. The conservative approach to deducting cleaning equipment would be to claim your Time-Space percentage of the cost. If you can say that the primary reason for renting the equipment is because of the business, take the assertive position and deduct the full amount. (See the section on House Expenses on page 93 for a discussion of how to deduct the cost of renting an apartment.)

REPAIRS AND MAINTENANCE OF PERSONAL PROPERTY

Some general comments: Costs associated with making repairs on your personal property that are caused by your business are fully deductible. For example, a child damages your microwave or VCR and it costs $75 to repair it. You may deduct $75 as a business expense. If your own child caused the damage you could deduct your Time-Space percentage of $75. (See the section on House Repairs and Maintenance on page 93 for a discussion of how to claim expenses for repairs and maintenance on your house.)

If you hire someone to come in and clean your rugs or to do your laundry (cleaning service, diaper service, dry cleaners, or launderer), you may deduct at least part of the cost as a business expense. If you take the assertive approach you would claim 100% of these costs by arguing that they are primarily for your business. (If you hire someone to clean your home, deduct this as a House Expense. See Chapter 5.)

Below are examples of business expenses to include under the category of repairs and maintenance of personal property.

Cleaning
    Air fresheners
    Baby wipes
    Bath towels/bath mats
    Bleach
    Broom
    Cleansers
    Clothes hamper
    Clothes iron
    Clothespins
    Diaper service
    Dishwasher detergent
    Dustmop
    Dustpan
    Electric dustbuster
    Fabric softener
    Furniture polish
    Hand towels
    Kleenex tissue
    Laundromat costs
    Laundry and cleaning service
    Pail or bucket
    Paper towels
    Rug cleaner
    Scouring pads
    Soap - hand, dish, laundry
    Sponges
    Stain removers

Cleaning (cont'd.)
    Toilet bowl cleaner
    Toilet paper
    Toothbrush and toothpaste
    Vacuum cleaner
    Vacuum cleaner bags
    Washcloths
    Wastebasket
    Wet mop
    Window cleaner

Repairs
    Repairs of personal property (furniture, appliances, toys, etc.)
    (See page 93 for a discussion of house repairs.)

Maintenance
    Candles
    Flashlight
    Flashlight batteries
    Pest control
    Salt for water softener
    Service contracts on appliances (washer, dryer, stove, refrigerator, microwave)
    Window shades

SUPPLIES

For all the items listed below, you may claim 100% of the cost if they are used exclusively for your business. If they are also used personally you may deduct your Time-Space percentage of the cost. If you use some items more than your Time-Space amount, you may claim a higher percent based on your actual business use, but keep some record of how you determined your actual business use.

Children's Supplies
  Art and craft supplies
  Backpack
  Baby intercom system
  Baby swing, walker
  Baseball, football, basketball, soccer ball, tetherball, jump rope, frisbee, skateboard
  Bib
  Birthday and holiday cakes and catered food

  Birthday and holiday presents: You may deduct up to $25 per person per year for gifts. You may give presents to the parents of the children you care for as well. Although you may spend more than $25 in gifts on one person, the maximum deduction is $25. You may want to take an assertive position and claim that some presents are actually entertainment expenses for group parties and celebrations.

  Blocks
  Board games
  Booster seats
  Brushes
  Chalk, chalkboard
  Changing pad

Children's Supplies (cont'd.)
  Charcoal
  Children's aprons
  Children's books
  Children's furniture: stove, chair, sink, refrigerator, etc.
  Clay
  Collage material
  Construction paper
  Cots
  Crayons
  Cribs with mattresses
  Diaper pail
  Disposable diapers
  Dolls
  Dress-up clothes
  Dry markers
  Easel
  Fabric
  Field-trip fees: zoo, museums, parks, etc.
  Flannel board
  Floor mats
  Glue
  Headphones
  High-chair

  Holiday celebration decorations: Christmas, Chanukah, Halloween, Valentine's Day, St. Patrick's Day, Easter, Independence Day, etc.

Children's Supplies (cont'd.)
- Homemade toys
- Infant seats
- Magnifying glass
- Mattresses
- Milk deliveries
- Mirrors
- Mobiles
- Monthly children's curriculum (*Kapers for Kids, Little People's Workshop, Kaleidoscope Curriculum,* etc.)
- Music box
- Musical instruments: triangle, bells, drum, recorder, guitar, tambourine, maracas, xylophone, kazoo, harmonica
- Napping mats
- Paint/paintbrushes
- Paper
- Party favors, decorations, and balloons
- Paste
- Pegboards
- Plastic crates
- Playpen
- Potty chair
- Presents purchased for your own children but used by the children in your care
- Props for pretend play
- Puppets
- Puzzles
- Rattles
- Records, tapes, video tapes
- Riding toys
- Roller skates, ice skates
- Sand-and-water tables
- Scissors

Children's Supplies (cont'd.)
- Small toys
- Songbooks
- Stencils
- Stickers, labels
- Stuffed animals
- Tempera paint
- Thermometer
- Tissue paper
- Wading pool
- Wagon
- Walkers, strollers
- Water toys
- Windchimes
- Yarn

Kitchen Supplies
- Aluminum foil
- Baking dishes
- Beater
- Blender
- Bowls
- Cookbooks
- Cookie sheets
- Cookie cutters
- Cooking timer
- Cutting board
- Dish towels
- Dishes
- Electric can opener
- Food processor
- Garbage bags
- Garbage can
- Glassware
- Knives
- Matches
- Measuring cups and spoons
- Mixer
- Napkins
- Paper plates and cups
- Plastic bags
- Plasticware

Kitchen Supplies (cont'd.)
  Plasticwrap
  Popcorn popper
  Potholders
  Pots and pans
  Serving dishes

Kitchen Supplies (cont'd.)
  Silverware
  Tablecloth
  Tupperware
  Utensils
  Waffle iron

TAXES AND LICENSES

If you pay payroll taxes for your assistants (social security, medicare, federal unemployment, state unemployment, workers' compensation, etc.), you may deduct their full cost. Any licensing fees you incur to become licensed (fees to the social service department, medical exams and X-rays, zoning permits, fire or health department fees) are 100% deductible. You may deduct all the sales taxes on business purchases, but it is easier to include them in the cost of a purchase rather than separating them out. (See the section on House Expenses on page 92 for a discussion of how to deduct real estate taxes.)

TRAVEL, MEALS, AND ENTERTAINMENT

If you travel away from your home overnight to a family child care conference or for some other business activity (camping trip, workshop, etc.), you may deduct the full cost of the travel (standard mileage rate or actual expenses for the car, car rental, airplane, bus, train, taxi, etc.) and your lodging. You may only deduct 80% of your food and entertainment costs while on a business trip. Or, instead you may claim $26 a day for a standard meal allowance for most areas in the United States ($34 a day in higher cost-of-living areas). No receipts are necessary to claim this standard allowance. Travel to Alaska and Hawaii are not covered by this standard allowance. See the *Family Child Care Tax Workbook* for further details. If you attend a workshop or meeting for business purposes and return home for the night, you may claim the food you ate only if you are eating with other providers or parents to talk about your business. If so, you may deduct 80% of the cost of the food you purchase at this business event. You are always entitled to claim your mileage costs for any business travel.

TELEPHONE

You may not deduct as a business expense the monthly cost of the first telephone line in your home. This is true even if you installed the phone as a requirement to be licensed. If you purchase a second phone line for your business, you may deduct 100% of this cost. The following telephone related costs are deductible: long-distance business calls; services such as call waiting, call forwarding, and custom ringing; fees for the repair of the phone or phone lines; separate business listing in the White Pages; or a Yellow Pages advertisement. You may also deduct a portion of the cost of purchasing the house phone or a cordless phone. (Use your Time-Space percentage unless you purchased a separate phone primarily for your business.)

WAGES

Many providers pay outside assistants to work with the children. Are such assistants your employees or independent contractors? The difference between the two has major tax implications. If you have an employee you may have to withhold social security tax, medicare, and federal income tax, and pay federal unemployment and the employer portion of social security tax. You may also have to withhold certain state taxes. If you hire an independent contractor, you do not withhold or pay any taxes on the amount you pay someone, but merely deduct what you pay them as a business expense. Do not report payments to independent contractors on the "Wages" line of **Schedule C.** If you do, the IRS will presume you have an employee.

What is an employee? According to the IRS, "Anyone who performs services is an employee if you, as an employer, can control what will be done and how it will be done. This is so even when you give the employee freedom of action. What matters is that you have the legal right to control the method and result of the services." It doesn't matter if you agree to call the other person an independent contractor or whether the employee works full- or part-time.

Anyone working for you who helps you care for the children should be considered an employee, no matter how little she works for you. You certainly control what work this employee will do and how it will be done. The difference between an employee and an independent contractor can be illustrated by using the example of a plumber and a child care assistant.

	Plumber		Child Care Assistant
1)	Uses his/her own tools.	1)	Uses your house and its contents (toys, supplies, equipment, etc.).
2)	Works under his/her own direction as to when, where, and how the work is done. You tell the plumber about the problem and he/she fixes it without any instruction from you about how to disconnect a pipe.	2)	Works under your direction and instruction. You tell the helper how you want the children treated and what activities there will be.
3)	Implies no continuing relationship with you.	3)	Has an ongoing work relationship with you and the children.

People who come into your home on special occasions to perform specific services for you are not typically considered employees. Someone who comes in and cleans your home for your business, or occasionally repairs your toys, or presents a special magic show or activities program for the children is not your employee. These people aren't working under your specific control or direction and should be considered independent contractors. Someone who is in the business of providing back-up care, serving as an assistant to several providers besides you, is more likely to be an independent contractor.

If you are using an independent contractor in your business, put your agreement in writing. Make sure that it says that the person you hire is not an employee and that the person will not be eligible for unemployment compensation. You should also stipulate that the person will be responsible for her or his own income taxes. Such a written agreement is not conclusive evidence that you do not have an employee. The IRS requires that you file a **Form 1099 - Misc: Miscellaneous Income** if you pay any one independent contractor more than $600 each year. There is a penalty for not filing this form if you are required to do so. For more information, see the *Family Child Care Tax Workbook.*

An important note: Many family child care providers do not consider their assistants to be employees, even though they meet the IRS definition of employee. The IRS is becoming more active in enforcing the rules in this area. Although filing the proper forms and paying the proper withholding taxes can be frustrating and difficult to understand, it is recommended that you take the time to do this correctly. There are penalties for taxpayers who do not file these forms properly and on time. If the IRS rules that you had employees, it will hold you responsible for all back taxes, including the employer and employee share of social security and medicare.

Although you must treat those you hire to help you care for the children as employees, as a practical matter this is not always enforced by the IRS. For small amounts of money, say $100 per person in a year, the IRS is unlikely to bother you about withholding taxes and paying social security. You could also take the view that even if the IRS did audit you and declared that you had employees, the penalties and interest on $100 are not very much. You might decide that it is easier to take this small risk rather than trying to file the many tax forms.

If you are concerned that these withholding rules and the filing of a variety of tax forms is confusing and bothersome, you might consider using a payroll service for small businesses. Look under "bookkeeping services" in the Yellow Pages. These services can do all the withholding and prepare all the checks for your employees at a relatively low cost. Contact your local provider association to see if it might negotiate a special rate from a local payroll service. The cost to use such a service is fully deductible.

Hiring your own children or your spouse

You may pay your own son or daughter to help you in your business. If your child is under age 18 the amount you pay is subject to federal income tax but not social security, medicare, or federal unemployment tax. If your child is age 18 or older, the money paid is subject to all employer and employee taxes, including federal unemployment (if the child is over age 21).

If you hire your own child, there are three major issues to keep in mind:

1) The work must be directly related to your business. Your child may help you with cleaning, cooking, and (if a teenager) working with the children.
2) Your child must be capable of doing the work. There is no minimum age to be able to hire your child. The amount you pay your own child must be "reasonable." Use as a guide what you would pay another child from the neighborhood of the same age to do similar work. Your five year old can't be paid $6 per hour to clean the playroom.
3) Make sure you keep careful records that enable you to distinguish payments for business work from your child's allowance. An allowance cannot be used as a business deduction. You can keep records by marking your calendar or notebook when your child works for you and noting what work is done. For example:

MARCH

S	M	T	W	T	F	S
	1 cleaning 1 hr	**2**	**3** cleaning 1 hr FIRE DRILL DAY ASH WEDNESDAY	**4**	**5**	**6**
7	**8** cleaning 1 hr	**9**	**10** cleaning 1 hr	**11**	**12** cleaning 1 hr	**13**
14	**15** cleaning 1 hr	**16**	**17** cleaning 1 hr ST. PATRICK'S DAY	**18**	**19**	**20** SPRING BEGINS
21	**22** cleaning 1 hr	**23**	**24** cleaning 1 hr	**25**	**26**	**27**
28	**29** cleaning 1 hr	**30**	**31**			

Total for March:
10 hours worked X $4.25 per hour
= $42.50.

Paid on March 31.

Either write a check to your child or, if paying cash, write a receipt that shows what was done for the money.

228306

Customer's Order No.   Date 3/15 1993

Name _Allison_

Address

SOLD BY	CASH	C.O.D.	CHARGE	ON ACCT	MDSE. RETD	PAID OUT

QUAN.	DESCRIPTION	PRICE	AMOUNT
	For child care work – cleaning		
	10 hrs x $4.25hr = $42.50		
	pd. 3/15 cash		
	Sally Provider		

ALL claims and returned goods MUST be accompanied by this bill.

Rec'd by

76

If you pay your child as an assistant, your child must fill out **Form W-4** (to claim an exemption from withholding). You must file **Form 941: Employer's Quarterly Tax Return** to report that wages were paid, and you must issue a **Form W-2** and **Form W-3** at the end of the year to report annual wages paid. Finally, you need to obtain an employer identification number (**Form SS-4: Application for Employer Indetification Number**) to use on all your business tax forms. Your children must report the money they earn from you to the IRS by filing their own **Form 1040: U.S. Individual Income Tax Return** at the end of the year. But because individuals must earn more than approximately $3,000 of income (see the *Family Child Care Tax Workbook* for the latest number) before owing any taxes, most children who work for their provider-parents will not have to pay taxes on this income. A final note: check with you state to determine if there are any state labor laws which may affect your ability to hire your own children for your business.

If you hire your spouse, remember that your spouse must report the money as income and pay taxes on it as wages. For this reason, there is a limited tax benefit in hiring your spouse. (You can deduct the employer share of Social Security and Medicare as a business expense.) See the *Family Child Care Tax Workbook* for details about the forms to fill out if you are hiring employees or family members.

A more important potential tax benefit in hiring your spouse is to purchase health and dental insurance, and other employee benefits for your spouse and deduct these as business expenses. Purchasing a family medical insurance policy for your employed spouse means that you and your children could be covered under the plan. There are some limitations to such plans. Your spouse must be doing work for your business. Consult an insurance agent for details.

IN-HOME PROVIDERS

An in-home provider is someone who cares for children in the home of the parent. In this situation, you would probably be considered the employee of the parent, and as such you should have federal unemployment taxes and part of your social security taxes withheld from your paycheck by the parent. You would report your earnings as income on the **Form 1040**. As an employee you are not a self-employed person and you would not fill out a **Schedule C**. In addition to these federal taxes, your employer may have to pay state unemployment and workers' compensation taxes. See the *Family Child Care Tax Workbook* for more information about employers and employees. See also **Circular E: Employer's Tax Guide** from the IRS.

OTHER EXPENSES

Below are some expenses that may be listed on separate lines under "Other Expenses" on your **Schedule C**.

Food

Keeping track of food expenses can be the most difficult record keeping task a provider will face. Because it is probably your single largest expense, food is often the target of IRS audits. It is important to carefully record food expenses so you can claim the highest, most accurate business deduction. If you are participating in the Food Program, be prepared to educate the IRS auditor about the fact that you will commonly serve food that is not reimburseable by the Food Program and that this food (popsickles, potato chips, birthday cake, etc.) is deductible as a business expense.

Recording food expenses is complicated and can easily get very frustrating. To illustrate this, let's look at an example:

You cook a dish of lasagna and the ingredients cost $4.00. You serve the lasagna for lunch to four children you care for, two children of your own (who are not on the Food Program), an assistant, and yourself. That night your family eats the leftovers. How much of that $4.00 is a deductible business expense? Only the amount that the four children ate, plus 80% of the amount that the assistant ate. What you, your children, and your family ate is not deductible. (For more information about the rule that only 80% of food served to assistants is deductible, see the *Family Child Care Tax Workbook*.)

How can you possibly keep track of food expenses under such rules? It is not easy. Here is a four-step process that you can follow to make sense of the rules and claim the proper food deduction:

Step One: Save all business and personal food receipts

It is not enough to just save receipts for your business. IRS **Publication 587: Business Use of Your Home** asks you to save family food receipts as well. When you and your spouse go out to dinner on Saturday night, save the credit card slip, the canceled check, or the receipt. I have talked to a provider who had $3,000 of business food receipts but had trouble in an audit because she had no personal receipts. The IRS didn't believe that all $3,000 was business expenses. Saving personal receipts for comparison will make your business claim seem more realistic.

Ideally, you should have these food records:
    1) Check stubs or canceled checks to show you spent money;
    2) Food store receipts to show that food was purchased;
    3) Copies of your menus to show that you prepared the food; and
    4) Attendance records to show that children ate the food.

Do you have to have all of these records? Probably not. But it is a good idea to have at least several weeks of complete records for all of these items. Food store receipts are the most important to save for the entire year. If you are on the Food Program, try to keep copies of the menus and attendance records that you turn in to your sponsor. The more food records you have, the better your chance of justifying your deduction. Try to get into the habit of saving receipts for even the smallest of items such as spices, flour, ketchup, mustard, soy sauce, baking soda, etc. These small items will add up to higher business deductions. Since you will be accumulating so many food records throughout the year, make sure you have a safe place to store them. You may want to staple together weekly or monthly receipts or store them in a marked manila envelope.

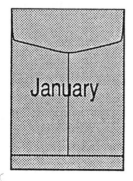
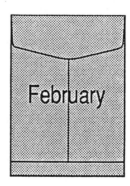
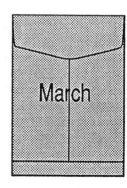

**Step Two: Separate business and personal food expenses,
where possible**

The most fundamental principle of food record keeping is to be able to show
the IRS that you know the difference between food used in your business
(which is deductible) and food used by your family (which is not). The
following tips are not required, but they can help make things easier: buy
food separately, cook food separately, use your business checkbook to pay
for the food used in your business, separate your food into business and
personal use by asking the checkout worker to subtotal this food on your
receipt, store food separately, etc. For many providers, following this advice
may not be practical. Don't worry. Just do what you can to keep track of the
food used in your business.

Step Three: Mark all food-receipt items as either business or personal

It is not enough to save food receipts. You need to mark on the receipt
whether each item is for business or personal use. The best time to do this
is when you are unloading your food from your grocery bags after returning
home from the grocery store. Each item on the receipt can be labeled in one
of four categories:
　　　　1) 100% business food;
　　　　2) 100% personal food;
　　　　3) Non-food; or
　　　　4) Shared business and personal food.

If you purchase some special snack food for the children or you know that
the second gallon of milk is for your business, mark these items as 100%
business. Personal food such as beer, wine, cigarettes, and steak cannot be
deducted, so mark them as 100% personal. Don't include paper plates,
plasticwrap and aluminum foil and other non-food items with your food
deductions. Mark these items and add them to your supply expenses by
claiming either your Time-Space percentage or an actual business-use
percent of these items for your business. Shared business and personal food
expenses are those used by both your family and your business (eggs, juice,
potatoes, cheese, flour, etc.).

Use a different color marker to label these categories or use abbreviations
such as "B," "P," "NF," and "S." Since many of the items will be in the "shared"
category, you may want to leave these unmarked to save yourself some time.

Let's look at how you might mark some sample receipts:

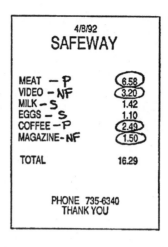

By marking your food receipts you are providing yourself with additional evidence to support your claim of deductible food expenses.

Step Four: Calculate a typical weekly average for business food expenses

This last step is the toughest. There are many methods for calculating business food expenses, and I will describe several. The IRS does not require any particular form of record keeping. But whichever method you use, make sure you have a clear, reasonable explanation for your calculations.

Family child care providers can have very different food habits. Some providers serve elaborate meals and encourage children to eat as much as they can. Other providers shop for bargains and use many newspaper and magazine food coupons. The number of meals and snacks served can vary. Because of this, I believe that it is important for a provider to be able to demonstrate to the IRS what her particular food habits are. To do this you need to be able to show exactly what the children you care for eat in a typical week.

Here's a way to do that: pick several different weeks throughout the year (at least three or four). Look at your menus, recipes, and receipts for these weeks and do a very careful job of pricing all the food that was eaten by the children. Start with the breakfast on Monday morning and continue through the last snack on Friday afternoon. Subtract any food eaten by you, your children, or your family. Let's look at a sample day of food records:

Provider has four children (ages 3,4,5, and 5) and one child of her own (age 3).

Receipt

1-1-92	
MILK-GAL	2.40
BREAD	1.49
GRAPE JUICE	1.94
BANANAS	1.49
MUFFINS	2.16
MEAT	4.28
PEANUT BUTTER	1.98
CHEESE	2.28
COFFEE	2.58
BAKED BEANS	.94
FRUIT COCKTAIL	1.27
NOODLES	1.65
APPLESAUCE	1.96
CRACKERS	2.14
TOTAL	$28.56

MONDAY

	Food	Am't Served	Am't of Purchase	*Am't Claimed
Breakfast	Milk	5 cups	$.75	$.60
	Bananas	1/2 bunch	.75	.65
	Muffins	all	2.16	1.90
Lunch	Milk	5 cups	.75	.60
	Cheese	1/2 of total	1.14	.90
	Baked beans	all	.94	.80
	Fruit cocktail	all	1.27	1.00
	Noodles	1/2 of total	.82	.70
Snack	Grape juice	1/2 of total	.97	.75
	Apple sauce	all	.96	1.50
	Crackers	1/4 of total	.54	.40
	Total food		$11.05	
	Total business food			$9.80

*Remember, this provider should not count the cost of the food that she and her own child eat.

Obviously, your calculation of how much was eaten by the children you care for is an estimate. Don't worry about being exact to the penny. The important point is to be able to show that you recognized that not all the food you served was deductible. As long as you are being reasonable, you will not have any trouble.

Let's continue with our example above and say that after doing several weeks of calculations, we come up with an average weekly business expense of $56.25. If you were open for 50 weeks in the year, you would claim a food expense of $2,812.50 ($56.25 X 50).

As a final check, go back to your marked receipts and add up the amounts you have under each food category. Let's say this was your result:

$525.46   100% business
$720.38   100% personal
$4,782.91   shared
$6,028.75   TOTAL FOOD

−$2,812.50   estimated business food
$3,216.25   ESTIMATED PERSONAL FOOD

Using our estimate of $2,812.50 as our business deduction, we can now see if this number is consistent with our yearly receipts. If our 100% business and shared receipts don't total at least $2,800, we know we made a mistake. Either our weekly-average estimate was too high or we did not save all of our receipts. In our example, you would say to yourself, "Is $3,200 a reasonable amount for my family food expenses?" If so, you are done with your calculations. If something doesn't seem right, you may want to make some adjustments.

Question: How do I account for food I purchased before I began doing child care?

You probably do not have receipts for food on your pantry shelves that you purchased before you started your business and then used in your business. Save any canceled grocery store checks of these purchases, if you can. To the best of your memory, make a list of these food items and their cost. Such items might include dry cereal, canned goods, and frozen food. Go ahead and claim the cost of these items served to the children. Not having receipts for these items should not create a problem for you.

Other Methods of Calculating Your Business Food Expense

As I said above, there is more than one way to come up with a reasonable estimate for your food expenses. No matter which method you choose, remember to save all your food receipts – both business and personal.

1) Instead of calculating an average weekly cost, take the time to mark every food receipt with your best estimate as to what percent of each food item will be eaten by the children in your care. After a few weeks, you should have an educated guess about the eating patterns of the children. Your receipts will look something like this:

```
┌─────────────────────────────────┐   ┌─────────────────────────────────┐
│           7-5-92                │   │           8-23-92               │
│                                 │   │                                 │
│ MILK-GAL — 100% Bus.    2.25    │   │ RAISINS - 100% Bus.     1.10    │
│ CORN  ⟩ Shared          .94     │   │ CHEESE  ⟩ Shared        2.34    │
│ CEREAL                  1.61    │   │ EGGS                    1.50    │
│ COFFEE — Personal       2.25    │   │ BACON — Personal        1.79    │
│ NAPKINS — Non food      .79     │   │ SPICES — Shared         .82     │
│                                 │   │ SODA POP — Personal     2.49    │
│ TOTAL              $7.84        │   │                                 │
│                                 │   │ TOTAL              $10.04       │
└─────────────────────────────────┘   └─────────────────────────────────┘
```

After a month or two of this, calculate a weekly average and use this to estimate your annual cost.

2) Calculate an average cost for your typical meals and snacks. Choose three or four weeks of menus and price out the meals and snacks. Use your attendance records for the whole tax year to tabulate how many children ate these different meals and snacks. For example:

	Breakfasts	Lunches	Snacks
Child #1	250	250	500
Child #2	100	125	250
Child #3	100	125	250
Child #4	0	100	100
Child #5	0	100	100
Child #6	250	200	300
TOTALS	700	900	1,500
Average cost	X $.95	X $1.10	X $.62
	$665	$990	$930

TOTAL FOR YEAR: $2,585

This method is more accurate if you have part-time children or if the number of children varies significantly from one part of the year to another.

3) If you are single and have no children of your own, it may be easier to calculate how much you eat and claim the rest as a business expense.

4) If you can reasonably estimate what portion of the total food each person eats, you can claim a single percentage of your total food expense as a business deduction. For example:

Provider	20%
Provider's spouse	10%
Provider's son: 6 years	10%
Child in your care: 5 years	10%
Child in your care: 4 years	10%
Child in your care: 6 years	10%
Child in your care: 4 years	10%

Children cared for: 40% X $6,000 (yearly food bill) = $2,400 business deduction

If you are using this method, you should have some evidence to back up how you arrived at your percent for each person. Showing how many meals in the year each person ate might be useful.

Question: How do I deduct the cost of growing or hunting food?

You may deduct all the costs associated with growing, preparing, and storing food for your business, but not the value of the food that is grown. For example, if you decide to grow green beans in your back yard, the following could be considered as business expenses: the cost of the seeds or starter plants, fertilizer, mulch, water, garden gloves, hose, hoe and other tools used to cultivate the plants, material to tie up the plants, bushel basket to put the ripe beans in, electricity or gas to cook the beans, freezer bags, and the freezer to freeze the beans. However, if you grew one bushel of green beans and this is worth $20 at the farmer's market, can you deduct $20? No. The value of the food is not deductible. If your own family eats some of these beans, you may only claim the portion of the costs associated with growing, preparing and storing the food that corresponds to the percentage of the beans eaten by the children in your care.

Early Childhood Education Center
Concordia University
7400 Augusta
River Forest. IL 60305
94-68

If you hunt for food and serve this food to your children, may you claim the expenses associated with the hunting? Yes, within reason. Some providers may hunt deer or other animals and serve the meat to children in their care. In such cases, reasonable costs such as the hunting license, gun shells, and mileage may be allowed. These expenses must be prorated based upon how much of the meat is used for business. If the costs associated with hunting exceed the value of the meat obtained, the IRS may decide that it is not a reasonable business expense. Use your judgment before claiming such expenses.

Note: Some local regulations prohibit providers from serving hunted meat to children. Although I do not recommend that you violate regulations, if you do serve such meat, it is still deductible as a business expense.

WHAT SHOULD I DO IF THE YEAR IS OVER AND I HAVE NO FOOD RECEIPTS?

You have several options. Let's say it is January. Carefully reconstruct your prior year expenses as accurately as you can and claim the amount you arrive at. Look at menus you used during the year. Reconstruct a typical week or month of menus. Go to the store now and price out the cost of the items necessary to serve these menus. Save any attendance records you have and calculate how many meals and snacks you served. Estimate the cost of serving these meals and snacks by using the prices you have obtained for the menus. Get statements from parents saying how often their children were fed during a normal day. Save any CACFP records as evidence of food served. Put down on **Schedule C** your best estimate based upon this calculation. Write out on paper everything that you used to make your estimate. Save all your calculations so you can show them if you are audited several years later. The more you can back up a reasonable estimate with your own calculations, the better off you are.

Although there is no standard meal rate that the IRS will accept as a business expense, you could use the Child and Adult Care Food Program reimbursement rate to help you estimate your food expenses for a previous year. Calculate how many meals and snacks you served for the previous year. Multiply these numbers by the Food Program reimbursement rates for that year for each meal and snack. This should only be done as a last resort. You could use this method even if you were only on the Food Program for part of the year, or not at all. The IRS does not appear to be challenging providers who show food expenses equal to the Food Program reimbursement rate. Be warned, however, that not all auditors will agree and that the practice could change without notice.

Remember, it is never too late in the year to start saving food receipts. Some receipts are always better than no receipts. Try to improve each year and reach the goal of saving all your receipts.

Household Items

Any item purchased to make your home more accessible to a disabled child or parent

Bath mat
Bathroom scale
Bicycles
Blankets, sheets, pillows, pillow cases
Booster seat, car seat

Cable TV fee, Disney Channel, etc. (Deduct the cost of these items according to the percentage of time you use your TV in your business.)

Camping equipment
Children's thermometer
Clocks
Extension cords
Film for a camera, film development
Fire extinguisher
Fireplace fixtures
Flowers/flower boxes
First-aid kit
Medicines
Mirrors
Nightlight
Indoor or outdoor thermometer
Pet muzzle
Safety barriers
Safety caps for electrical outlets
Safety locks and racks for firearms
Safety locks for medicine and poison
Shelving
Sleeping bags
Smoke detectors
Space heater
Storage containers
Tools: hammer, nails, screw drivers, saw, ladder, etc.
Umbrella
Wall posters
Window shades

Yard Supplies

Bug killer
Firewood
Garden hose
Gas for lawn mower
Gloves
Hoe
Lawn maintenance service
Lawn mower
Lawn sprinkler
Rake
Sand/sand box
Saw
Shovels
Snow removal service
Weed killer
Wheelbarrow

Other

Fees for field trip activities: admission charges for museums, amusement parks, zoos; costs for swimming lessons, gymnastics, etc. (Don't include any fees or charges for your own children, but do include expenses for yourself or a helper, and for the children in your care.)

Chapter 5: HOUSE EXPENSES

House expenses are those incurred to keep and maintain your home from year to year. If you don't own a home, you can still claim the business portion of any expenses you pay, such as rent, utilities and renter's insurance. Providers may take the business portion (Time-Space percentage) of the cost of these items as a business deduction each year. In 1991 a new tax form, **Form 8829: Expenses for Business Use of Your Home** was introduced for providers to use to record these expenses. All of the following expenses are to be entered onto **Form 8829:**

> Casualty losses
> Mortgage loan interest
> Real estate taxes
> House insurance
> House repairs and maintenance
> Utilities
> House rent

There is a limit as to the amount of these house expenses you can deduct each year. You cannot show a loss for your business by claiming these house expenses. (The exception to this rule is that you can always claim the Time-Space percentage of your mortgage loan interest and real estate taxes. See below for further details.) You will be able to tell if you are entitled to claim the business portion of all of these house expenses when you fill out **Form 8829** at the time you file your tax return. The instructions to **Form 8829** will explain how much of these expenses are deductible. (See also the *Family Child Care Tax Workbook* for details.) If you cannot deduct some of these expenses in one year, you can carry them forward as expenses to claim in the next year.

CASUALTY LOSS

A casualty loss is damage, destruction, or loss of property resulting from an identifiable event that is sudden, unexpected, or unusual. Examples: earthquake, tornado, flood, storm, vandalism, fire, or car accident. If your home or car insurance completely covers such damage, you don't have a business expense. If your insurance policy has a deductible of $250, and you pay this amount, you have a business expense. Your casualty-loss expenses must be adjusted by your Time-Space percentage, unless the damage was done to property that was used exclusively or to a large degree by your business.

Let's look at an example: A storm damages your home and property. All but $1,000 of the damage is covered by insurance. Your Time-Space percentage is 25%. If the property was used by your business and by your family, you could claim $250 as a business expense ($1,000 X 25%). If $500 of the property damage was to your furniture that was used exclusively for your business, you could deduct $500, plus $125 ($500 of the remaining property X 25%). If your business-use percent of damaged property was 75%, you could deduct $750 ($1,000 X 75%). Related expenses you have due to a casualty or theft, such as for the treatment of personal injuries, for temporary housing, or for a rental car may be deductible as business expenses. See **Publication 334: Tax Guide for Small Business** for further details.

MORTGAGE LOAN INTEREST AND REAL ESTATE TAXES

You are always entitled to claim the Time-Space percentage of your mortgage loan interest payments and your real estate taxes each year. The amount of these expenses you do not deduct for your business may be claimed on your **Schedule A**, if you itemize. Let's take an example, where your Time-Space percentage is 30%:

	Total yearly expense 100%	Schedule C expense 30%	Schedule A expense 70%
Mortgage loan interest	$3,000	$900	$2,100
Real estate taxes	$4,000	$1,200	$2,800

You must divide these expenses between **Schedule C** and **Schedule A** based on your Time-Space percentage. You cannot decide to claim them all on **Schedule A** because you want to show more expenses on this form. Actually, you are better off having as much of these expenses as possible on **Schedule C** because they will reduce your net business income, which is taxed at a higher rate (when social security tax is included) than your personal income.

HOUSE INSURANCE

House insurance protects you for damage to your home. If you rent, renter's insurance would be included here. All other insurance policies (liability, disability, medical, and automobile) are not lumped with the house expenses described in this section. These other policies may or may not be allowable as business deductions. (See the section on Insurance on page 64.)

HOUSE REPAIRS AND MAINTENANCE

House repairs and maintenance expenses are for the routine upkeep of your home in order to prolong its useful life: painting, wallpapering, patching walls, repairing broken windows, fixing screens, sanding floors, fixing light fixtures, cleaning or repairing the furnace, purchasing service contracts on your built-in appliances, carpet cleaner, floor polish and wax, plunger, light bulbs, etc. They would also include staining an outdoor deck, replacing broken roof shingles, fixing a plumbing leak or a frozen pipe, removing lead paint, and replacing blown electrical fuses. (This category does not include repairs and maintenance of your personal property. See page 68 for a discussion of claiming repairs and maintenance on personal property. Personal property repairs are listed directly on **Schedule C**, where there is no limit as to how much of such expenses may be claimed each year. House repairs and maintenance are listed directly on **Form 8829** where there is a limitation each year as to how much of these expenses may be claimed.)

An important note: There is a difference between house repairs and major home improvements. House repairs merely keep your home's present value; major home improvements increase the value of your home and must be depreciated over a number of years. (See page 104 for a description of how to claim major home improvements.)

UTILITIES

Utilities include gas, electricity, water, sewage, and trash-removal expenses. Claim the Time-Space percentage of these expenses, unless you can show you spent a higher percent for business.

HOUSE RENT

If you rent your home or apartment, you may claim the Time-Space percentage of the rent. If you rent and pay for your own utilities, you may also deduct the Time-Space percentage of this expense.

CHAPTER 6: CAPITAL EXPENDITURES

Capital expenditures are those items used in your business that will last longer than one year. As a rule of thumb, the IRS usually will not treat an item costing less than $100 as a capital expense. For example: a stroller that costs $125 should be treated as a capital expenditure, but a tape recorder that costs $70 would be a direct business expense (as described in Chapter 4).

Below are the categories of capital expenditures for your business. The rules on how to deduct these expenses for your business may be different for each category:

House
Major home improvements
Land improvements
Personal property
Automobile

In most instances, capital expenditures cannot be deducted as business expenses in one year. Since these items gradually wear out over time, they are deducted as expenses over a predetermined number of years; this process is called *depreciation.* Tax laws require providers to depreciate their capital expenditures. See the *Family Child Care Tax Workbook* for complete information about how to apply the current depreciation rules when you are ready to file your tax return.

Below is a depreciation worksheet that you may wish to use to keep track of your capital expenditures. It is filled in with some examples to show how it may be used. A blank copy of the worksheet that you may copy can be found in Appendix C.

DEPRECIATION WORKSHEET

DESCRIPTION OF PROPERTY	MONTH/YEAR PUT INTO BUSINESS USE	PRICE*	BUSINESS USE %**	BUSINESS BASIS***
HOUSE ($50,000 – $5000 land = $45,000)	1/1/93	$45,000	30%	$13,500
MAJOR HOME IMPROVEMENTS				
New furnace	8/10/93	$1,500	30%	$450
LAND IMPROVEMENTS				
Fence	9/4/93	$1,100	30%	$330
PERSONAL COMPUTER				
ENTERTAINMENT, RECREATION OR AMUSEMENT ITEMS				
TV	1/1/93	$150	10%	$15
VCR	1/1/93	$100	10%	$10
ALL OTHER PERSONAL PROPERTY ITEMS				
Sofa	1/1/93	$250	30%	$75

*Price: For all expenditures except the house, list the fair market value or purchase price, whichever is lower. To arrive at the price of the house, take the purchase price minus the value of the land at the time of purchase. Add to this the cost of any major home improvements made before your home was used by your business.

**Business-Use Percent: For the house, major home improvements, land improvements and other personal property, use your Time-Space percentage or an actual business-use percent. For a personal computer and entertainment items, use an actual business-use percent, not your Time-Space percentage.

***Business Cost Basis: Multiply the Price for each item by the amount of the Business-Use Percent column. The Business Basis represents the amount you will be able to depreciate for each item. To find out how much of the Business Basis can be taken as an expense each year, see the *Family Child Care Tax Workbook*.

GENERAL RULES ABOUT DEPRECIATION

The rules concerning depreciating capital expenditures are complex, and Congress has regularly changed them over the years. Once you begin depreciating an item under a particular rule, however, you must continue depreciating it under that rule, even if the rules change in later years. Therefore, whenever you start depreciating an item (such as a refrigerator), save a copy of the depreciation schedule that shows how many years you must depreciate the refrigerator and how much you can deduct in each year. You will follow this schedule as long as you own the refrigerator.

What if you discover that you should have begun depreciating an item in a previous year (such as your home) when you were in business, but you didn't? You have three choices:

1) Don't do anything about depreciation and lose any chance of claiming a business deduction for the item.

2) File an amended tax return and recalculate your taxes for the earlier year. You can go back as far as three years after filing your tax return to file an amended return. By adding your depreciation expenses to your tax return from earlier years, you will reduce your taxable income and receive a refund. Use **Form 1040X: Amended U.S. Individual Tax Return.**

3) Don't file an amended return, but start depreciating the item in your current year, based upon the rules that were in effect when you first used the item for your business. In doing so you will lose the depreciation deduction for the earlier years. For example: You started your business in 1991, but you haven't depreciated your home. It is now 1993. You could start depreciating your home in 1993, but 1993 represents the third year of depreciation for your home. You must follow the 1991 depreciation rules for determining how much you can claim in 1993, as the third year. If you don't file an amended return for 1991 and 1992, you will lose the depreciation deductions for these years. If many years have passed and you haven't claimed any depreciation for an item, it may be too late to claim anything in the current year. Ask the IRS or your tax preparer what the depreciation rules were for earlier years.

MID-QUARTER CONVENTION RULE

If you purchase more than 40% of your capital expenditures (excluding your home and major home improvements) in the last three months of a year, your depreciation deduction will be reduced for that one year. This mid-quarter convention rule will affect providers who begin caring for children in the last three months of the year. After the first year you are entitled to claim the full depreciation deduction. For further details see the *Family Child Care Tax Workbook*.

CATEGORIES OF CAPITAL EXPENDITURES

HOUSE

Every provider is better off financially by depreciating her house. Do not listen to anyone who tells you that you shouldn't depreciate your house. There are two important reasons for taking depreciation for your house (1) By taking the depreciation you will reduce your taxable income each year you are in business; and (2) Any higher taxes you may have to pay later because you used your house in your business will be the same whether you claimed depreciation expenses or not.

Let's look at an example to illustrate this second point:

Purchase price of home (1987)	$165,000
House depreciation for 5 years	-$2,000
Adjusted basis of home (1992)	$163,000
Sale price of home (1992)	$175,000
Profit on sale of home (1992)	$12,000

You used your house for child care for five years and claimed $400 each year as a house depreciation expense. You later sold your home at a profit of $10,000. To this profit you must add the amount of depreciation you claimed, to arrive at a total of $12,000 in profit. What if you did not claim the $2,000 worth of depreciation expenses over the five years you were in business? You would still have a total profit of $12,000. Why? Because the IRS says that if you were *entitled* to claim house depreciation, it will treat you as if you did claim it. So, because you will have the same profit later whether or not you claimed depreciation, you are always better off claiming house depreciation while you are in business. (See page 100 for a further explanation of the consequences of selling your home.)

HOW TO DETERMINE THE BUSINESS COST BASIS OF YOUR HOME

The business cost basis of your home is the amount that can be claimed as a business expense over the years through depreciation.

1) Start with the purchase price of your home. If you built part or all the home yourself, count only the amount you paid for materials, not the value of your or your spouse's labor. Subtract from this the value of the land at the time you bought it. Land is not depreciable. (Ask your local property tax assessor for the value of your land when you purchased your home. If you can't get this value, use the current proportion of land and house values to calculate the value of your land when you bought your house. For example: You bought your house in 1985 for $150,000. Today your house is worth $170,000 according to your property tax statement. Check your property tax statement or call your property tax assessor's office for an estimate of the value of your land today. Let's say your land today is worth $17,000. $170,000 ÷ $17,000 = 10%. Ten percent of the purchase price of your home is the approximate value of your land in 1985. $150,000 X 10% = $15,000.)

2) Add to this adjusted purchase price the cost of any major remodeling or home improvements (room additions, new siding, outdoor deck, etc.) done to your house before you went into business. Do not count minor repairs such as painting, wallpapering, sanding floors, and plumbing. (See page 104 for an explanation of the difference between a major home improvement and a home repair.)

3) Multiply this new total by your Time-Space percentage. (See page 50 for an explanation of how to calculate your Time-Space percentage.) The result is the business cost basis of your house.

Let's look at an example:

$150,000	Purchase price of house in 1985
-15,000	Value of land in 1985
135,000	Adjusted purchase price
+3,500	Outdoor deck installed in 1987
138,500	Basis of home
X 25%	Time-Space percentage in 1992 (year you entered the business)
$34,625	Business-cost basis of house for 1992

4) Determine over how many years, and what rules you must use, to depreciate your house. See the *Family Child Care Tax Workbook* for details. If you have begun to depreciate your home in earlier years, continue using the same depreciation rules you used in previous years. Do not change time periods once you have begun to depreciate your house.

This business-cost basis of your home may change each year if your Time-Space percentage changes. Otherwise, the basis of the home ($138,500 in our example) will never change.

Selling Your House

Providers should be aware that selling a house can have major tax consequences. I strongly recommend consulting a tax attorney or professional tax adviser before putting your home on the market.

I explained above that house depreciation will increase the taxable profit of your house once it is sold. (Remember, this is true even if you didn't *claim* the depreciation you were entitled to!) In addition, if you sell your house while you are in business, you must recognize the gain of the business portion of your home in the year of the sale. Normally, if taxpayers who sell their house buy another one of greater value within two years of the sale, they can postpone paying any tax on all the gain to a later time. But, as a family child care provider who is in business when selling your home, you cannot postpone paying tax on the business portion of this gain. If you have gone out of business before selling your home, you may be able to postpone paying tax on all the gain to a later time.

Let's look at an example:

This example reflects a very simplified explanation of how to calculate the cost basis of your home when you sell it. I have not included costs such as land, selling expenses, closing costs, moving expenses, etc. The example should only be used for comparison purposes to illustrate the effect of being in the child care business when you sell your home. Taxpayers age 55 and older who are filing joint returns and who have lived in their homes at least three of the five years before selling, may exclude up to $125,000 of gain on the sale. This may be taken only once in a taxpayer's lifetime.

TAX CONSEQUENCES OF SELLING YOUR HOUSE

	Taxpayer #1 If you are a taxpayer who has not used your home in business.	Taxpayer #2 If you are in the child care business when you sell your home and your Time-Space percentage is 25%.		Taxpayer #3 If you used your home in the child care business but are out of business when you sell your home.
		75% Personal	25% Business	
Selling price of old home	$150,000	$112,500	$37,500	$150,000
Basis of old home (purchase price of $130,000 plus $10,000 improvements)	$140,000	$105,000	$35,000	$140,000
Total house depreciation claimed because of doing child care	0	0	-$3,000	- $3,000
Adjusted cost basis of old home	$140,000	$105,000	$32,000	$137,000
Gain on sale	$10,000	$7,500	$5,500	$13,000
Gain not postponed	0	0	$5,500 (pay tax on $5,500 as ordinary income in year of sale)	0
Gain postponed (no tax is owed in year of sale)	$10,000	$7,500	0	$13,000
Purchase price of new home, costing more than old home, bought within 2 years of selling old home	$160,000	$160,000 ($160M)		$160,000
Basis in new home	$150,000 ($160,000 - $10,000)	$112,500 ($160M x 75%) =$120,000 – $7,500=$112,500)	$40,000 ($160M x 25%)	$147,000 ($160,000 - $13,000)
Sale of new home when you are age 55 or older	$274,500	*(if not in business)* $274,500		$274,500
Minus cost basis in home	$150,000		$152,500 ($112,500 + $40,000)	$147,000
Profit on sale	**$124,500** *No tax on profit if you elect to use the $125,000 rule*		**$122,000** *No tax on profit if you elect to use the $125,000 rule*	**$127,500** *Pay tax on $2,500 if you elect to use the $125,000 rule*

Notice a couple of things in this example:

1) Taxpayer #2 paid tax on $5,500 when she sold her old home because she was in business when she sold it.

2) Taxpayer #3 was able to postpone paying any tax on the sale of the old home because she was not in business when she sold it. But she had to pay tax on $2,500 on the sale of her new home because when the house depreciation was added to her profit, it exceeded the $125,000 limit.

Obviously, if you are not in business when you sell your home, you can avoid paying some taxes by being able to postpone all the gain from the sale of your home. How long must you have been out of business before you sell your home? The IRS says that if you went out of business in an earlier tax year than when you sold your home, you could postpone the gain. But if you go out of business in the same tax year as you sell your house, you would need to prove that the decision to go out of business was unrelated to your decision to sell your home. The IRS will not allow you to postpone the business gain if they think you went out of business merely to avoid reporting the business income.

Because the amount you may have to declare as income from the business portion of the gain of your home may be substantial, it is a good idea to plan and seek professional assistance before selling your home.

Will it make any difference if you don't claim any house depreciation in the year of sale? No, you would still have to report your business gain. But, if you planned, you could take steps to reduce your Time-Space percentage (use fewer rooms in your home or work shorter hours) and thus reduce the amount of your business gain.

REFINANCING YOUR HOME

When refinancing or buying a home, be sure you understand that by lowering your mortgage interest payments you will reduce the interest deductions you may claim for your business. Additionally, you'll need to know how to depreciate the costs associated with the refinancing. Here are some things to keep in mind:

The cost of either the interest or the use of the money (sometimes called "points") must be "spread" (amortized) over the life of the loan. Divide these costs by the number of years the new loan is for, and then deduct the Time-Space percentage. Use this formula whether you pay the points up front or add the points to the amount of the loan. For example: Your interest charge is $1,500. The new loan is for 15 years. Your Time-Space percentage is 30%. Divide $1,500 by 15 and multiply that amount ($100) times 30%. Your business deduction each year for your interest is $30.

You'll also want to depreciate the costs associated with processing the new loan. These costs include title insurance, appraisal fee, credit report, state deed tax, and mortgage registration fee. Then, when you sell your home, add these costs to the basis (purchase price) of the new home when you figure the profit. For example: On January 1992 the closing costs for your loan total $1,000. Multiply $1,000 by your Time-Space percentage (30%) to get $300. Depreciate $300 over 31.5 years (see IRS **Form 8829** to find the depreciation percentage for each year). The first year of depreciation would be $9.13 ($300 X 3.042%).

An understanding of how the costs of refinancing will affect your loan– and the amount of your mortgage payments– will help you feel confident about your decision whether or not to refinance.

MAJOR HOME IMPROVEMENTS

Major home improvements increase the value or add to the life of your home. They include such things as room additions, new storm or screen windows or doors, new roof, new garage or shed, siding, outdoor deck, remodeled kitchen or bathroom, new ceiling fan or light fixture, new wall-to-wall carpeting, new built-in cabinets, garbage disposal, security system, and new vinyl flooring.

There is a difference between a major home improvement and a house repair. A repair merely protects your house's current value. Examples of repairs include painting, plumbing, electrical wiring, and replacing broken windows. Repairs can be deducted in one year. Major home improvements must be depreciated over a number of years, after multiplying the cost of the improvement by your Time-Space percentage. For example: $4,000 for an outdoor deck X 25% Time-Space = $1,000 business cost basis for depreciation. See the *Family Child Care Tax Workbook* for details about the current depreciation rules.

You could use your actual business-use percent instead of your Time-Space percentage in calculating the depreciation of your major home improvement. It makes sense to do this if your business-use percent is much higher than your Time-Space percentage. Be advised, however, that you will need to maintain some evidence to support your claim for a higher business-use percent. It would probably not be possible to claim a higher business-use percent for home improvements that are an integral part of the home: new roof, new windows, or siding.

If you make repairs as part of extensive remodeling or restoration of your home, the entire job is an improvement. For example, if you paint the walls in your bathroom, it is a repair that can be expensed in one year. However, if you painted the bathroom walls as part of the bathroom renovation project, you would have to add the cost of painting to the total renovation cost and depreciate the total.

If you have begun depreciating a home improvement from a previous year, continue using the same depreciation rules you started with. If you didn't depreciate a home improvement from a previous year, you may pick up the depreciation in your current year, according to the rules that existed the year you first completed the improvement. You may also file an amended tax return to claim depreciation from an earlier year. (See page 113 for a further explanation.)

LAND IMPROVEMENTS

A land improvement is an expense that increases the value of your property that will remain attached to the land after you leave. Examples of land improvements include a fence, sod, landscaping, new trees and shrubs, new driveway, built-in sand box, basketball or volleyball stand, patio, septic tank installation, and play equipment such as a swing set or jungle gym that is permanently attached to the land.

To claim these expenses you would multiply the cost by your Time-Space percentage to determine the business cost basis. This result can then be depreciated over a number of years. The *Family Child Care Tax Workbook* describes the most current depreciation rules.

Again, you may want to use your actual business use percent instead of your Time-Space percentage in calculating the amount of your depreciation deduction. This may make sense for a fence that you install for your business when you have no young children of your own, or if you can show that the use of the item is mostly for your business. For example: You estimate that the children you care for use the sand box 80% of the time. If so, you can depreciate 80% of its cost.

PERSONAL PROPERTY

Personal property refers to those items used in your business that are not attached to either your home or land. Most providers will have and purchase a significant amount of personal property that will make it worth their while to keep accurate records and depreciate these expenses. There are three categories of personal property with different depreciation rules for each category:

> 1) Personal computer,
> 2) Property used for entertainment, recreation, or amusement, and
> 3) All other personal property.

Consult the *Family Child Care Tax Workbook* for complete information on the current depreciation rules for each category of personal property.

Personal Computer

This category also includes a printer, printer stand, and computer table. You must keep track of how much time your personal computer is used in your business (for children's games, business record keeping, menu planning, etc.) and how much time for personal purposes. Divide the number of hours of business use by the total number of hours of use. Do not use your Time-Space percentage for this. Try to keep several weeks of records, at least, that may look something like this:

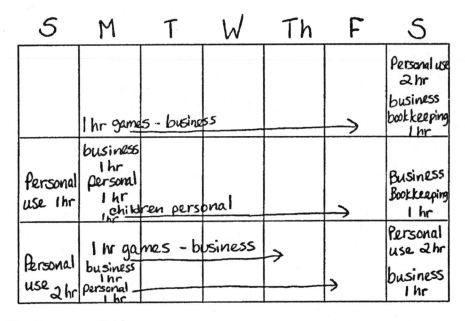

Business use: 14 hours
Personal use: 19 hours
Total hours used: 33 hours
Business-use percent: 42.4% (14/33)

Property Used for Entertainment, Recreation, or Amusement

This category includes items such as TV, VCR, video recorder, camera, record player, radio, piano and other musical instruments, tape recorder, etc. You must keep track of how much time you use each of these items for your business in the same way you do for a personal computer, keeping a log as described and shown above. Do not use your Time-Space percentage for these items.

All Other Personal Property

This last category of personal property includes all personal property not already covered in the first two categories. Items that are attached to the home, such as built-in appliances, are depreciated as either part of the house or a major home improvement. Remember the general rule that personal property items costing less than $100 can be deducted as a business expense in one year. Personal property items that must be depreciated if they cost more than $100 and will last longer than one year include:

Beds
Bookcases
Chairs
Chests
Clothes dryer
Coffee tables
Couch
Dehumidifier
Desk
Dining-room table and chairs
Dishwasher
Draperies, curtains
Dressers
End tables
File cabinets
Freezer
General furniture
Lamps
Lawn furniture
Lawn mower

Mattresses
Microwave
Outdoor play equipment
Picnic table
Power tools
Refrigerator
Rocking chairs
Room air conditioner
Rugs, carpets
Sewing machine
Snow blower
Sofa
Space heater
Stove
Stroller
Swing set
Tables
Washing machine
Water softener

Before you can depreciate these items as business expenses, you must first determine how much of their cost can be attributed to your business. For items that are used 100% for your business, you may depreciate 100% of their cost. Some providers have rooms in their homes that are used strictly for business. If so, 100% of the cost of every item of personal property that is purchased for that room may be depreciated for the business. Be careful not to claim a 100% business use of any purchase that is used by your own children in the evenings or on weekends.

If the personal property you purchased has both business and personal uses, you have two choices of how to determine the business expense that may be depreciated. Most providers will apply their Time-Space percentage to the cost of personal property purchases. This is clearly the most convenient method to use. Your second choice is to calculate an actual business-use percent for the item. You may want to use this method for items that are used for business at a much higher rate than your Time-Space percentage.

Determine the actual business-use percent by dividing the number of business hours the item is used by the total number of business and personal hours the item is used. If you choose this method, you should keep some record of your calculations to be able to back up your number if questioned by the IRS. It will be up to you to prove that your figure is accurate, but you don't have to keep a log every day showing business use. Perhaps several weeks of logs will be enough. The higher your business use percent, the more evidence the IRS may ask you to show as justification.

Let's look at an example: You buy a swing set in 1992 for $1,000. Your Time-Space percentage is 25%. If you used the Time-Space percentage you would depreciate $250 of the cost of the swing set ($1,000 X 25%). But you could determine that the children you care for use the swing set 10 hours a week (2 hours per day X 5 days) and your own children use it an average of 7 hours a week (1 hour per day X 7 days). Your business-use percent would be 59% (10 hours of business use divided by 17 hours of total use). You would depreciate $590 of the cost of the swing set ($1,000 X 59%). Since 59% business-use is significantly greater than your 25% Time-Space percentage, it may be worth it to use the business-use percent.

At the end of the year, a list of all the personal property items that you purchased might look like this:

100 % Business items		Time-Space % items		Actual business use items
double stroller	$125	clothes dryer	$350	freezer (75%)
file cabinet	$100	lawn mower	$200	$250 X 75% =
	$225		$550	$187.50
		X 30% T/S = $165		

The rules concerning how to depreciate these totals each year are found in the *Family Child Care Tax Workbook.*

Previously Purchased Personal Property

The process just described is to be used for personal property items you purchase in one year and start to depreciate in that year. What about items that you purchased before you went into business? This section will discuss the situation of a provider in the first year of business. The following section will cover providers who have been in business longer than one year.

When a provider first starts to care for children there are many items of personal property used by her business in her house that were purchased before the business began. Providers are entitled to claim a portion of the cost of these items as business expenses. Many providers overlook these items and thus miss out on a significant source of tax deductions.

Providers must depreciate the cost of items that were purchased before the business began, even if the value is very small. For example: A provider who buys a toaster for $45 after going into business could deduct her Time-Space percentage of the toaster cost in one year. If the toaster was bought before the business began, however, it must be depreciated. To determine how to claim expenses for personal property items purchased before the business began, follow these steps:

Step One: Take a large note pad and conduct an inventory of all items of personal property in the house that are used on a regular basis for the business. List each item by room or area of the house. Include items in the basement, garage, and outdoor shed.

What items should be included in your list? A provider using the conservative position would only count larger items and those items used directly by the business. A provider using the assertive position would count all items in a room that help create a "home-like" environment for children. Consider this: What you are selling to parents is your personal services in your home. The environment and appearance of your home is very important to parents. The parents are expecting it to be maintained as a home. If you decided to take down all the pictures off your living room and dining room walls, parents would probably not approve of this change because it would make your home less "home-like." Mirrors, clocks, wall pictures, and other home decorations provide stimulation for children and help create a warmer environment. Without these items, your home would be less stimulating to children and you would probably attract fewer parents. You should be reasonable in deciding what to include in your inventory. It is probably not appropriate to include fine china, antiques, expensive oil paintings, or items that are not seen by children on a regular basis. Let's look at an example of an inventory of items in a living room and bedroom (where children take naps every day) using the conservative and assertive positions:

Conservative Position	Assertive Position
	(Includes everything on the conservative list, plus these additional items)
Living Room	Living Room
couch	clock
stuffed chairs (3)	mirror
coffee table	wall pictures (3)
lamps (2)	fireplace fixtures
rug	picture frames
bookcase	sideboard
	books in the bookcase

Bedroom	Bedroom
bed frame	blankets
mattresses	sheets
rug	pillows/pillowcases
lamp	clock
	wall pictures (3)
	dresser
	bedside table

As you can begin to see, your inventory of personal property could easily add up to hundreds of items.

Conducting such an inventory is also useful to do for insurance purposes in case you ever suffer a loss because of theft, fire, or storm damage.

Step Two: Estimate the fair market value of each item at the time you began using it in your business. What could you get for each item if you were to sell it at the time you went into business? Do not use the cost of replacing the item. A sofa purchased in 1988 for $600 might only be worth $200 in January 1992. To save time you can lump items together before estimating their fair market value. Use your best judgment when estimating. For more expensive items, you may want to take pictures for your records. Better yet, rent a video recorder and take a home movie of the rooms in your home. If you do so, the cost of renting the recorder and the video tape are fully deductible. If you put the video tape in a safe deposit box with other personal items, part of the cost of the box is deductible. Multiply the cost of the safe deposit box by your actual business-use percent and deduct the result as a business expense. Your inventory list for your kitchen might now look like this:

<u>Kitchen</u>

refrigerator	$500
microwave	$100
stove	$200
small appliances (toaster, blender, electric can opener)	$50
table	$50
chairs (4)	$40
pots and pans (50)	$250
glasses (25)	$50
silverware (80)	$40
utensils (30)	$30
dishware (50 plates, bowls, cups, saucers, etc.)	$50
cookbooks (15)	$30
Tupperware storage containers (10)	$30
serving bowls (4)	$40
baking utensils (15 cookie sheets, baking dishes, etc.)	$30
aluminum foil, wax paper, etc.	$5
other items (15)	$30
	TOTAL: $1,525

Step Three: Divide your inventory list into three categories: personal computer; property used for entertainment, recreation, or amusement; and all other personal property. The rules for depreciation are different for each category. (For the first two categories follow the explanation on pages 105 to 106.)

Step Four: For all other property, determine how much each item was used for business purposes. If the item is used 100% for business purposes, use 100% of the fair market value for depreciation. If the item has both business and personal uses, most providers will find it easiest to apply their Time-Space percentage to the fair market value. You could also calculate an actual business-use percent if you can back up your claim with some record.

After following this last step, your inventory list for items in your basement and garage might look like this:

<u>Basement/Garage</u>

100% business use items

children's bicycles (3)	$150
outdoor toys (2)	$50
stroller	$60
TOTAL: $260 ———————▶	$260.00

Time-Space percent items

clothes washer	$150
clothes dryer	$150
clothes hamper	$10
lawn mower	$60
snow blower	$75
freezer	$50
household tools (30)	$300
garden tools (10)	$100

TOTAL: $895 X 30% T/S = $268.50

Actual business-use items

refrigerator $100 X 60% =	$60
shelves $30 X 60% =	$18
TOTAL: $78 ———————▶	$78.00
	TOTAL: 606.50

Total amount of items in the basement/garage that may be depreciated: $606.50. To determine how to depreciate these expenses, consult the *Family Child Care Tax Workbook.*

Question: What if I have been in business for more than a year and have not yet begun to depreciate my personal property?

You have three choices:
1) *Don't do anything about claiming depreciation and lose all the deductions for these items.*
2) *File an amended tax return and recalculate your taxes as far back as three years.*
3) *Don't file an amended return, but start depreciating these items in your current year based upon the rules that were in effect when you first began using each item for your business. In doing so you will lose the depreciation deduction for the earlier years.*

Is it worth it to file an amended return to begin picking up a few years of depreciation on personal property items? The answer depends upon your willingness to reconstruct your records. Personal property expenses could easily total several hundred dollars in business deductions each year. You must estimate the fair market value of these items at the time you first began using them for your business. If you have been in business for more than seven years, the depreciation timeline may have expired and you will not be able to claim any more depreciation expenses. (See below for a further discussion about claiming depreciation in this situation.)

Keeping Track of Personal Property Depreciation Over the Years

The most difficult part of depreciating personal property items is conducting the inventory and calculating the deduction for the first year. After the first year it is easier to claim these expenses. Here are several important points to help you after the first year:

1) If the item wears out before the end of the depreciation period, you may deduct the remaining unclaimed depreciation in the year that it wore out. Many of your household items will not last the full depreciation period, so you will be able to write off these items much faster than you may have originally planned.

2) If you buy a new item (such as a TV to replace an old TV), you would begin depreciating the new TV under the rules in effect for the year you bought it.

3) You may have an item around your home that you haven't used in your business, like a sewing machine. If you later begin using this sewing machine for your business, you may begin depreciating it starting the year it is used for your business. Use its fair market value when it was first put into business use.

4) If you quit the child care business before the end of the depreciation period for your personal property, you do not have to pay back any depreciation you have already claimed, unless you used accelerated depreciation or Section 179 depreciation rules. (See the *Family Child Care Tax Workbook* for details.) If you used straight line depreciation, you would simply stop claiming any more depreciation expenses. You would not be able to deduct the remaining unclaimed depreciation on these items. This rule is the same for house depreciation, major home improvements, and land improvements. If you quit the child care business in 1991 and then started up again in 1994, you would start depreciating your personal property using 1994 as year one. The basis of this property would be its fair market value in 1994.

5) If you sell your personal property, you may have to pay back some of the depreciation you deducted. See the *Family Child Care Tax Workbook* for details.

6) Keeping track of what depreciation rule you must follow for each personal property purchase over the years can be confusing. The following chart may help:

Keeping Track Of Depreciation Over The Years

This chart shows how to keep records for items depreciated beginning in 1992 using rules in effect that year: 7-year Straight-line depreciation (see the *Tax Workbook*). Be aware that the rules for depreciation for 1993 and after may change. This chart assumes that the 7-year straight-line rules do not change by 1996. Once you start depreciating an item under one rule, however, you must continue to follow the same rule for that item. Using such a chart may make it easier to keep track of your depreciation expenses. The Time-Space percentages shown are used merely as examples.

1992	1993	1994	1995	1996
Year 1 refrigerator	Year 2 refrigerator	Year 3 refrigerator	Year 4 refrigerator	Year 5 refrigerator
$800 X 25%=$200 X 7.14%=$14.28	$800 X 25%=$200 X 14.29%=$28.58	$800 X 25%=$200 X 14.29%=$28.58	$800 X 30%=$240 X 14.28%=$34.27	$800 X 30%=$240 X 14.29%=$34.30
	Year 1 swing set	Year 2 swing set	Year 3 swing set	Year 4 swing set
	$1000 X 25%=$250 X 7.14%=$17.85	$1000 X 25%=$250 X 14.29%=$35.73	$1000 X 30%=$300 X 14.29%=$42.87	$1000 X 30%=$300 X 14.28%=$42.84
		Year 1 clothes dryer	Year 2 clothes dryer	Year 3 clothes dryer
		$500 X 25%=$125 X 7.14%=$8.93	$500 X 30%=$150 X 14.29%=$21.44	$500 X 30%=$150 X 14.29%=$21.44
			Year 1 sofa	Year 2 sofa
			$700 X 30%=$210 X 7.14%=$14.99	$700 X 30%=$210 X 14.29%=$30.01
				Year 1 rug
				$200 X 30%=$60 X 7.14%=$4.28
Total: **$14.28**	**$46.43**	**$73.24**	**$113.57**	**$132.87**

Report your depreciation expenses on IRS **Form 4562: Depreciation and Amortization.** Notice that the depreciation deduction changes in 1995 when the Time-Space percentage rises from 25% to 30%. See the *Tax Workbook.* for further information.

AUTOMOBILE

A provider can only depreciate her car if she is choosing to use the actual-expenses method of claiming car expenses. Most providers will use the standard mileage rate method. (See page 60 for a further discussion of each method.)

Many providers believe that keeping track of the capital expenditures identified in this chapter is extremely difficult. It is to your benefit, however, to take the time to understand these rules and claim all allowable deductions. Use a tax preparer or ask the IRS for help, if necessary. Don't be concerned if it takes you several years before you are comfortable with the rules of depreciation.

CHAPTER 7: OTHER TAX ISSUES

ESTIMATED TAX

Many providers are not aware that they should be paying estimated tax, although most providers can avoid paying this tax by meeting one of many exemptions.

As a family child care provider, you are self-employed and do not have taxes withheld from your earnings throughout the year. Most wage-earning taxpayers pay income taxes throughout the year, and the IRS does not want to wait until the end of the year for you to pay all the taxes you owe. Generally, if you expect to owe $500 or more in federal income tax by the end of the year, you may be subject to paying estimated tax.

If you must make estimated tax payments, they are due four times a year: April 15, June 15, September 15, and January 15. To pay this tax you must estimate your yearly income and subtract your estimated yearly expenses. Next you should calculate your estimated taxes owed on this net profit. (Remember to include any social security taxes owed.) Pay in the first one-fourth of this tax by April 15. If your estimate of your income or expenses changes later in the year, you may adjust your next estimated tax payments.

There are four major situations in which you do not need to make estimated tax payments throughout the year:
1) If you know that you will receive a tax refund on your individual, joint or separate return.
2) If you or your spouse (if filing jointly) will have paid in at least 90% of your total tax bill throughout the year. For example: if your total tax bill is $7,000 for your family, you must have paid in at least $6,300 ($7,000 X 90%) throughout the year or else you will be penalized. To make sure you will meet this goal, ask your spouse to have more withheld from her paycheck. Your spouse would fill out a new **Form W-4: Employee's Withholding Allowance Certificate** and give it to her employer.
3) If you had no income tax liability in the previous year, or
4) Your family taxes withheld this year are greater than your taxes paid last year. Look at the taxes you paid for all of last year on your tax return. Let's say you paid $8,000 in taxes. If your family withholds at least $8,001 in taxes this year, you won't have to pay in quarterly estimated tax payments. Ask your spouse to make sure she has at least $8,001 withheld this year from her paycheck. A note of caution: Don't forget that while you may avoid having to pay estimated tax, you still may owe more taxes when you file your tax return.

To file estimated tax you must send in quarterly **Form 1040-ES Estimated Tax for Individuals**. For specific instructions on how to fill out this form, see the *Family Child Care Tax Workbook*.

SOCIAL SECURITY (SELF-EMPLOYMENT) TAX

Self-employment tax is the tax that entitles you to social security benefits. All family child care providers who have a net profit of $400 or more from their form **Schedule C** are required to pay this self-employment tax. The amount of social security benefits you will receive after you retire are based in part on the taxes you pay. To receive social security benefits, you or your spouse must pay into the social security fund. Family child care providers, especially women who have not worked much outside the home, can make sure that they will qualify for social security by paying self-employment tax, even if it means reducing their expenses to declare at least a $400 net profit. File Form **Schedule SE Self Employment Tax** when you file your **Schedule C**. Consult the *Family Child Care Tax Workbook* for the current tax rate.

SHOWING A PROFIT

If you are doing child care with the intention of making a profit, you are entitled to deduct all ordinary and necessary business expenses. If a loss results, you can use this business loss to offset other income on your personal tax return. If you aren't trying to make a profit, the IRS will rule that you have a hobby and will disallow your business deductions. If you report a profit for your business three out of every five years, the IRS will presume that you are trying to make a profit. If you don't meet this test you can still claim losses if you can show the IRS that you are taking reasonable steps to try to make a profit.

Most family child care providers should not worry that the IRS will treat their business as a hobby because they will have little trouble showing that they are working long hours and trying to be successful. Many providers show losses during their first year or two because of equipment purchases and low enrollment. This is perfectly acceptable. Don't refuse to show a loss simply because you are afraid the IRS will audit you.

IRA's AND SIMPLIFIED EMPLOYEE PENSIONS

As a self-employed business owner, you should be planning ahead for your retirement. If you set aside money in an Individual Retirement Arrangement (IRA), you can reduce your current taxes and save money for the future. You can set aside up to $2,000 a year in an IRA account. You cannot deduct for your IRA more than your net profit for your business, up to a maximum of $2,000. In other words, if your net profit (gross income minus business expenses) is $1,500 for your business, you can deduct up to $1,500 for an IRA. If your net profit is $2,000 or more, you can deduct up to $2,000 for an IRA.

If you are not covered by a retirement plan but your spouse is covered by a plan at work, you may be further limited as to how much you can deduct for an IRA. See IRS **Publication 590: Individual Retirement Arrangements** for details. You must make your contribution for an IRA by April 15.

If your net income for your business is greater than $2,000, you may want to look at setting up a Simplified Employee Pension (SEP) which allows you to set aside more money for your retirement. Under a SEP plan, you can contribute up to 13.0435% of your net income or $30,000, whichever is less.

You may set up a SEP plan even if you do not qualify for an IRA because your family income is too high or because your spouse is already covered by a pension plan. If you already have an IRA, setting up a SEP plan may reduce the amount of contributions you can make to your IRA.

You can invest your SEP plan funds in virtually the same type of accounts as an IRA. See a bank, broker, or financial adviser, or contact an investment fund for futher information. Money set aside in a SEP will reduce your federal income taxes. To set up a SEP, use the model SEP arrangement in **Form 5305-SEP.** You must make your contribution to a SEP plan by April 15.

For providers who want to contribute more to a retirement plan, setting up a Keogh plan may be advisable. A Keogh plan works like a SEP plan with a few exceptions:

1) You can contribute up to 20% of your net profit; 2) You must report annually to the IRS (**Form 550** series by July 31 of the following year, even if you made no contribution); and 3) you have somewhat less flexibility in determining how much to set aside.

You must open a Keogh plan by December 31, although later-year contributions may be made by April 15.

All providers should seriously consider setting up some type of retirement plan for themselves. It can be one of the best investments you will ever make.

INCORPORATING YOUR BUSINESS

Some tax preparers recommend that you incorporate your business in order to reduce your taxable income and reduce risks of liability. Before you consider such a decision, get a second opinion from a professional tax preparer or attorney. Find out if in your situation you will actually benefit from incorporation. Make sure to take into account these disadvantages of incorporating:

1) You must file a corporate tax return, and the cost of hiring someone to prepare this is usually more than preparing your **Schedule C**.
2) You will spend additional time on record keeping since corporate and personal funds can't be comingled.
3) The cost of setting up a corporation can run between $500 and $1,500 plus filing fees.
4) You will lose the chance to hire your own children, and your wages will be subject to any state unemployment compensation taxes.

CHAPTER 8: DEALING WITH TAX PREPARERS

The federal tax laws were not written with family child care providers in mind. Congress focuses most of its attention on more traditional small businesses. The tax code is often vague and only occasionally directly addresses family child care issues. Many tax preparers do not have much experience with family child care and therefore may overlook some rules or else give you incorrect information. Improve your chances of getting accurate help by following the steps outlined below.

WHEN TO GET HELP FROM A TAX PREPARER

An increasing number of providers are using tax preparers to help them reduce their tax liability. Under what circumstances should you consider using a tax preparer? There is no rule that says you should or should not hire one. If you are reasonably satisfied with your ability to understand the tax rules and follow the directions in filling out the forms, then perhaps you don't need further help.

On the other hand, if you are not confident about your knowledge of taxes, you shouldn't hesitate to ask for help. You can use a tax preparer to file your taxes for you or you may want someone to answer just a few questions on some key points. Here are some situations in which you might consider using a tax preparer:

- You are just starting out caring for children and you aren't sure what the federal and state tax requirements are for doing child care.
- You need help with the personal property depreciation rules covering furniture, appliances, and major purchases for your business.
- You are thinking about buying or selling a home.
- You realize that you did not claim some substantial business deductions in a previous year and you are thinking about filing an amended tax return (**Form 1040X**) to get a refund.
- You have done your own taxes for several years but now want to check to make sure you are doing everything correctly.

WHAT TO LOOK FOR IN HIRING A TAX PREPARER

Like any other significant financial decision, take the time to shop around and compare. Not all tax preparers are the same. Here are some key questions to ask:

1) What kind of training does the tax preparer have? Look for someone who is an Enrolled Agent (a credential issued by the IRS after the preparer passes a test), a Certified Public Accountant (CPA), a tax attorney or a tax preparer who specializes in family child care taxes. Ask what sort of ongoing tax training the person is taking in the area of small-business tax returns. Many commercial tax preparation agencies give their employees a limited amount of training, most of which involves individual income tax returns. They may know little about the business of family child care and still less about the deductions to which you are entitled. They will tend to be more conservative in preparing your return.

2) How many family child care tax returns did the tax preparer do last year? Although experience is an important quality, a less experienced preparer may have more energy for your business and keep up with changes in the law.

3) How many family child care tax returns signed by the tax preparer have been audited over the years? Was the preparer at fault in any of the audits? Although being audited is not necessarily a reflection on the tax preparer, you want to know if the preparer is doing returns correctly.

4) What does the tax preparer charge? Is the fee based on a flat amount per return or an hourly rate? If your tax return is complicated, a flat amount per return is usually preferable. Make sure you ask about all fees up front.

5) Do you feel comfortable with the tax preparer? Is the person easy to reach and talk to? You will likely maintain a better relationship with a tax preparer if you both share somewhat similar philosophies about taxes. If you are very conservative in claiming deductions, look for a preparer who understands you and will follow your wishes. Likewise, if you are more assertive in claiming deductions, find someone who shares your views.

HOW TO WORK WITH A TAX PREPARER

Be prepared to take some time with your tax preparer to explain the nature of your business. Some providers take a copy of this book and the *Family Child Care Tax Workbook*, both published by Redleaf Press, to their tax preparer to make sure he or she is aware of all the tax rules that affect providers. To help you screen tax preparers who may be uninformed about family child care, ask these questions:

1) Should I depreciate my home as a business expense? Answer: Yes, it is always better to take this deduction.
2) May I count in my Time-Space calculation the hours I spend cleaning my house because of my business, after the children are gone? Answer: Yes.

3) Do I depreciate my TV differently than my sofa? Answer: Yes. A TV is considered "entertainment" property and a sofa is considered "other personal property."

4) If I have a helper whose only job is working for me 20 hours a week, can I treat this person as an independent contractor? Answer: No, the IRS will treat all regular helpers as employees.

What if the tax preparer you are considering doesn't answer these questions correctly? If the preparer insists that the above answers are wrong, you will probably be better off looking elsewhere. But if the preparer is willing to spend the time to learn more about your business, you may be able to work together.

Remember that even if you are using a tax preparer, you still have the responsibility of keeping good records for your business. Before you mail your tax return to the IRS, make sure you understand everything that was done by the preparer. You are responsible for what is on your tax return. Ask questions of your preparer until you understand why the tax preparer made the calculations he or she did. If you are audited, and your tax preparer is unavailable, you will have to defend what your return says.

WHAT TO DO IF YOUR TAX PREPARER MAKES A MISTAKE ON YOUR RETURN

If filing an amended return will correct the error, and it is not too late to do so, ask the tax preparer to do this. The preparer should not charge for this service if it was his or her mistake. If you are paying penalties and/or interest because of your preparer's mistake, demand that the preparer pay these fees. You are always responsible for any income tax owed. If you no longer trust your tax preparer, hire someone else the next time.

HOW TO FIND A TAX PREPARER

Ask other local providers whom they use. Look in the Yellow Pages. Ask the provider association, your child care resource and referral agency, or a Food Program if they can refer someone to you. Some communities have taxpayer assistance services to help low-income people or other taxpayers in need. Contact your local United Way for more information about these programs. There are three national tax preparer organizations that may be able to make referrals. They are the National Association of Enrolled Agents, the National Society of Public Accountants, and the National Association of Tax Practitioners. Look in the phone book for a local chapter or call your local Chamber of Commerce.

CHAPTER 9: STICKING UP FOR YOURSELF WITH THE IRS

BE INFORMED

The best source of IRS information can be found in the various publications that are listed on page 130. If you have questions, call your local IRS office or visit if you want to have a longer conversation about a more complex problem. There is never a charge to receive advice from the IRS. What if the answer you get from the IRS is not clear or is different from what you have heard from this book or someone else? Ask the agent to refer you to a written reference in the tax code or an IRS publication that supports their position. If the IRS agent is unsure about the answer to your question, you can ask the IRS to research the problem and send you a written response. It will take at least several weeks to receive an answer.

You may also want an IRS speaker to come to a local meeting of providers to answer questions. Any Food Program, child care resource and referral agency, or provider association can invite someone from the IRS Taxpayer Service office. If you do, be very specific about what you want the speaker to cover. For instance, you might ask the person to talk about the Time-Space percentage, how to record food expenses, personal property and house depreciation, and how to treat assistants as employees. Have someone talk to the speaker ahead of time to make sure he or she understands what you want.

IF YOU ARE AUDITED

Many family child care providers are worried about what will happen if they get audited. Nationwide, less than 2% of all taxpayers who file a **Schedule C** will get audited each year. Your tax return can be chosen for an audit in several ways:
1) It is chosen at random by the IRS computer;
2) The IRS decides to look more closely at different types of businesses each year to learn more about what the typical business owner is taking as deductions, and they may choose family child care one year;
3) The IRS computer keeps track of average deductions by business type. If one of the deduction lines on your **Schedule C** is out of the norm, you may be subject to an audit. For instance, your gross income one year is $20,000 and your car expenses are $7,000. This is probably an unusually high car expense for this level of income. You are likely to be audited.

Your car expenses may, however, be totally allowable because you have all the proper records. It is not a good idea to lump many of your business deductions on one line (for example "Supplies"), because you run a greater risk of an audit.

When you are notified that you are being audited, the IRS may ask for supporting records for all your forms, for one form, or for just one line on one of your forms. The auditor may ask you to mail in your records or set up an appointment at his or her office or your home. IRS auditors do not all have the same experience. Some may be very familiar with the family child care business, others not at all. Here are some suggestions to follow if you are meeting with an auditor:

1) Bring in only those records that the agent asks for, nothing more. You don't want the IRS examination enlarged to cover other areas just because you accidentally showed the agent records about selling your car, for example. If the IRS wants more information, you can simply go home and bring back more records another day.

2) Don't volunteer information. Only respond to the specific question being asked. You can hurt your own case by saying too much and revealing facts about new subjects that the agent may not have known about.

3) Don't go into an audit alone. Bring along your tax preparer. (Some tax preparers will want you to stay home while they handle the audit without you. This can be effective, if the preparer is well informed about your tax return.) If you don't have a tax preparer, bring along your spouse, accountant, a friend, or an attorney. You need to have someone who can give you moral support and help you remember what was said. Often having a person who understands tax law with you will cause the agent to treat you more favorably.

HOW TO HANDLE DISPUTES WITH THE IRS

Most IRS audits are straightforward. You may have misunderstood the law, or the IRS didn't understand what you put on your return. The most common problem providers have is not keeping adequate business records. Most problems are usually quickly resolved. Many providers, just like many taxpayers, are intimidated by the IRS. An audit can be a frightening, demoralizing experience. But what should you do if you don't agree with what the auditor is saying? Here are some tips to help you stick up for yourself:

Just because an auditor says something is true doesn't make it so. Ask the auditor for written evidence of his or her position in the Internal Revenue Code, IRS publications, Revenue Rulings, Tax Court decisions, or some other written record. Insist upon seeing something in writing. Without written authority, the auditor is on shaky ground, and you should be able to argue your case with more confidence. Don't accept vague assurances that what the auditor is saying is true. Take this example: The auditor says, "You can't include hours you spend cleaning your home in your Time-Space calculation." You respond, "Where does it say I can't?" The auditor will not be able to find any written document supporting this position. In fact, there is a Revenue Ruling and a Tax Court decision that says you can include these hours. (See Chapter 3.)

Here is another example: The auditor says, "You can't deduct the cost of semi-monthly birthday parties because they aren't a requirement of doing child care." You respond, "Where does it say that I can't deduct something simply because it is not required by any regulations? I have many expenses that aren't required, such as advertising, association dues, books and magazines, etc. What is the difference between birthday party expenses and these items?" You are entitled to deduct all "ordinary and necessary" expenses for your business. Birthday parties certainly meet that standard.

Often providers get into trouble when an auditor says something like, "You can't take that deduction because you don't have adequate records," or "I'm not allowing this expense because it is really personal, not for your business." How can you respond to these statements? You should press the auditor to tell you exactly what you need to show to be able to claim the deduction. Ask "What kind of records must I have for you to accept this deduction?" or "How can I prove to you that this toy was only used for my business?" There must be some method of record keeping that is reasonable that the IRS will accept. If the auditor can't tell you what you can do to prove your case, don't accept the result.

Take this example: The auditor says, "I don't believe that 50% of your receipts for household supplies were actually used for your business. I'll give you 25% of these costs." You respond, "I have shown you my total receipts for supplies. My home is open for business about 40% of the time. I care for eight children and there are four members of my own family. I figure that with these facts I am using at least 50% of these supplies for my business. What other method should I be using to calculate the correct percent? What else do I need to do to prove to you that 50% is a reasonable number? What method did you use to come up with 25%?" If the auditor can't answer these questions to your satisfaction, don't give in.

3) Sometimes the auditor will try to tell you how you should run your business. The auditor may say, "Why do you take two trips to the grocery store each week? Can't you do all your shopping in one trip?" You respond, "I buy a lot of food each week and it is too difficult to carry home food unless I make several trips (or there's not enough refrigerator space, etc.). Besides, I prefer to shop twice a week because it gets me out of the house. I choose to run my business on my schedule. Shopping twice a week is not unreasonable."

Another auditor tells you, "I'm not going to give you two hours a day for cleaning because you should be doing some of your cleaning while the children are sleeping." You respond, "I don't wish to clean while the children are sleeping. Every worker is entitled to workbreaks and a lunch break. I don't have to do any work during that time. I use my breaks to relax. Why should providers be expected to work without breaks if no other worker is required to do so?"

An important note: The two situations described above in number 3 are not fiction. The provider who responded with the above arguments convinced the auditor to back off.

4) If you and the auditor can't get along, ask for the auditor to be replaced. If you believe the auditor is being unreasonable, ask to speak to the auditor's supervisor. You have a right to appeal any decision made by your auditor. The IRS must explain the process of appeal. See also IRS **Publication 556: Examination of Returns, Appeal Rights, and Claims for Refund.** There are no penalties for appealing. The IRS usually will not want to spend the time and money on an appeal, so it will likely try to compromise with you.

A final comment: IRS auditors can make mistakes or be unaware of how the tax rules affect your business. You should not be afraid to stand up for yourself and be assertive. Many providers have done so and have won their cases. If your position is a reasonable one, you should insist on being taken seriously until the IRS can show you some written document that verifies or clarifies their position. If you lose, you simply pay the taxes owed, plus any interest and penalties. If you win, you will reduce your taxes and have the satisfaction of sticking up for yourself.

A FINAL WORD

At first glance, much of this material may seem complex and confusing – so much so that you may feel you'll never "get it." Don't give up right away. Carefully read through this book several times until you understand it. Obtain and read carefully all the IRS instruction booklets that pertain to your tax situation. When tax time comes around, follow the instructions as faithfully as possible, and refer to the sample forms included as a guide.

No one person can ever begin to understand every detail of federal tax law – not tax preparers, tax lawyers, or even IRS officials – least of all, ordinary taxpayers. All that can be expected is that you keep complete, up-to-date records, follow tax instructions as best you can, and complete your tax forms honestly. You can do it.

SHARE YOUR TAXING EXPERIENCE WITH THE AUTHOR

Have you been audited by the IRS? What kind of experience was it? Did you agree with how the IRS treated your tax return? Have you argued with your tax preparer about whether something was deductible or not?

I am interested in hearing from providers about their experiences (both good and bad) with the IRS and tax preparers. I am collecting information to urge the IRS to clarify the tax laws and also to advocate changes in the Internal Revenue Code, where necessary, with elected officials. Write Tom Copeland at Redleaf Press, 450 North Syndicate Ave., Suite 5, St. Paul, MN 55104.

LIST OF IRS FORMS AND PUBLICATIONS
FOR YOUR FAMILY CHILD CARE BUSINESS

<u>Citation of forms in the text</u>

Schedule C, Profit or Loss from Business   11, 22, 24, 25, 53, 58, 63, 73, 78, 87, 92, 93, 118, 120, 125

Schedule SE, Self-Employment Tax   118

Form W-10, Dependent Care Provider's
        Identification and Certification   27, 28

Form 1040 ES, Estimated Tax for Individuals   118

Form 1040, U.S. Individual Income Tax Return   77, 78

Form 1040 X, Amended U.S. Individual Tax Return   97, 121

Form 2441, Child and Dependent Care Expenses   16, 32

Form 4562, Depreciation and Amortization   63, 115

Form 5305, Simplified Employee Pension   119

Form 8829, Expenses for Business Use of Your Home   50, 91, 93, 103

Publication 334, Tax Guide for Small Business   92

Publication 505, Tax Withholding and Estimated Tax

Publication 556, Examination of Returns, Appeal Rights,
        and Claims for Refund   128

Publication 583, Taxpayers Starting a Business

Publication 587, Business Use of Your Home   49, 55, 79

Publication 590, Individual Retirement Arrangements   119

Publication 917, Business Use of a Car

For employees:

Form SS-4, Application for Employer Identification Number   28, 77

Form W-2, Wage and Tax Statement   77

Form W-4, Employee's Withholding Allowance
        Certificate   77, 117

Form W-3, Transmittal of Income and Tax Statements

Form 940, Employer's Annual Federal Unemployment (FUTA)
        Tax Return

Form 941, Employer's Quarterly Federal Tax Return   77

Form 1099, Miscellaneous Income   24, 74

Form I-9, Employment Eligibility Verification

Circular E, Employer's Tax Guide   78

APPENDIX A

Part I. Rulings and Decisions Under the Internal Revenue Code of 1986

Section 262.-Personal, Living, and Family Expenses

If a taxpayer provides day care in the taxpayer's home, are the cost of basic local telephone service for the first telephone line provided to the home and other substantiated telephone charges deductible under section 262(b) of the Code? See Rev. Rul. 92-3, below.

Section 280A,-Disallowance of Certain Expenses in Connection with Business Use of a Home, Rental of Vacation Homes, Etc.

(Also Section 262.)

Calculation of the deduction for the business use of a home by day care providers. A day care provider should compute the amount of the deduction by treating a room as used for day care for the entire business day if it is available for day care use for the entire day and is regularly used for day care.

Rev. Rul. 92-3

ISSUE

How should a day care provider compute the amount of the deduction provided under section 280A of the Internal Revenue Code for the business use of the provider's home for day care during a taxable year?

FACTS

A, an individual, operates a full-time day care facility in A's home in state M. A is a licensed day care provider under the laws of M. A's day care business is regularly operated 11 hours each day (from 7 a.m. to 6 p.m.), five days a week, 250 days a year. During these business hours, A provides day care for several young children other than A's children. Some children arrive at A's home for day care at 7 a.m., and some do not leave A's home until 6 p.m. At any particular time during A's business day, A has at least 1 child(other than A's children) in A's home for day care.

The total floor area of A's home is 1,600 square feet. Although no rooms in A's home are used exclusively for A's day care business, several rooms in A's home are available for day care use throughout A's business day and are regularly so used as part of A's routine provision of day care. The total floor area of these rooms us 1,200 square feet. In addition, A spends on-one-half hour before and one-half hour after regular business hours preparing for and cleaning up after the children.

In addition to interest and taxes of $5,000, A, a calendar year taxpayer, incurred $4,000 of costs during 1991 for electricity, gas, water, trash collection, general maintenance, and insurance with respect to the use of A's home for day care and as a personal residence. The total depreciation for A's home during 1991 (determined under sections 167 and 168 as though the entire home were depreciable) was $1,000. Thus, A's total costs for 1991 were $10,000.

A's home has only one telephone line and A pays a monthly charge of $20 for basic local telephone service. The laws of M require A to have a telephone in order to be licensed by M to provide day care. A uses the telephone for both business and personal calls.

A has adequate records to substantiate the $10,000 of costs, the number of hours and days that A's day care business was operated (including preparation and clean-up time), the number of children for whom A provided day care, and A's telephone costs.

LAW AND ANALYSIS

Section 280A (a) of the Code provides generally that in the case of a taxpayer who is an individual or an S corporation, no deduction otherwise allowable shall be allowed with respect to the use of a dwelling unit that is used by the taxpayer during the taxable year as a residence.

Under section 280A(b), a subsection (a) shall not apply to any deduction otherwise allowable to the taxpayer without regard to the deduction's connection with the trade or business (for example, the deduction for qualified residence interest under section 163 and the deduction for state and local real property taxes on a personal residence under section 164).

Section 280A(c)(4)(A) of the Code provides, in part, that subsection (a) shall not apply to any item to the extent that the item is allocable to the use of any portion of the dwelling unit on a regular basis in the taxpayer's trade or business of providing day care.

Section 280a(c)(4)(B) of the Code provides, in part, that paragraph (a) shall apply only if the owner or operator of the trade or business has applied for, has been granted, or is exempt from having, a license, certification, registration, or approval as a day care center or as a family or group day care home under the provisions of any applicable state law.

Section 280A(c)(4)(C) of the Code provides, in part, that if a portion of the taypayer's dwelling used in the day care business is not used exclusively for day care purposes, the amount of expenses attributable to that portion shall not exceed an amount that bears the same ratio to the total amount of the items allocable to such portion as the number of hours that portion is used for such purposes bears to the number of hours the portion is available for use.

Section 280A(c)(5) of the Code, in part, limits the section 280A(c)(4) deduction for day care

expenses to the excess of the gross income derived from the day care business over the otherwise allowable deductions allocable to the day care business (e.g., interest and taxes) and the deductions allocable to that business that are now allocable to the use of the dwelling (e.g., food and supplies).

Section 262(b) of the Code provides that in the case of an individual any charge for basic local telephone service with respect to the first telephone line provided to any residence of the taxpayer shall be treated as a nondeductible personal expense.

In computing the deduction for a taxable year under section 280(A(c)(4) of the Code for the business use of A's home to provide day care, A should multiply the total costs incurred during the year with respect to A's home ($10,000) by two fractions. (If a rented rather than owned A's home, the amount of rent paid in 1991, rather than the depreciation, mortgage interest, and real estate taxes would be included in the costs incurred.) The first fraction is the total square footage in A's home that is available for day care used throughout each business day and that is regularly so used in that business, divided by the total square footage of A's home. The second fraction is the total hours in the year that the day care business is operated (including substantiated preparation and clean-up time), divided by the total number of hours in a year (8,760 hours). If a room is available for day care use throughout each business day and is regularly used as part of A's routine provision of day care (including a bathroom, an eating area for meals, or a bedroom used for naps), the square footage of that room will be considered as used for day care throughout each business day. A day care provider is not required to keep records of the specific hours of usage of such a room during business hours. Also, the occasional non-use of such a room for a business day will not disqualify the room from being considered regularly used. However, the occasional use of a room that is ordinarily not available as part of the routine provision of day care (e.g., a bedroom ordinarily restricted from day care use but used occasionally for naps) will not be considered as used for day care throughout each business day.

Thus, except as limited by section 280A(c)(5) of the Code, A may deduct under section 280A(c)(4) $2,568.49, which represents the portion of the $10,000 in expenses attributable to A's use of 1,200 square feet of A's home for day care for 3,000 hours (12 hours per day for 250 days) during 1991. The computation of the $2,568.49 day care deduction is as follows: (1200/1600) x (3000/8760) x $10,000 = $2,568.49. The nonbusiness portion of the otherwise deductible interest and taxes may be claimed as an itemized deduction.

Under section 262(b) of the Code, A's $20 monthly expense for basic local telephone service is a nondeductible personal expense, even though the state required A to have a telephone in order to be a licensed day care provider. Additional telephone charges incurred for business purposes are deductible under section 162 to the extent substantiated.

HOLDING

A day care provider should compute the amount of the deduction for a taxable year provided under section 280A of the Code for the business use of a home for day care by multiplying the total costs incurred during the year that are allocable to the use of the home by two fractions. The first fraction is the total square footage in the home that is available for day care use throughout each business day and that is regularly so used in that business, divided by the total square footage of the home. The second fraction is the total hours in the year that the day care business is operated (including substantiated preparation and clean-up time), divided by their total number of hours in a year. This deduction is limited as provided in section 280A(c)(5).

In addition, pursuant to section 262(b), no deduction is allowed for the cost of basic local telephone service for the first telephone line provided to the home.

DRAFTING INFORMATION

The principal author of this revenue ruling is Cynthia A. Davis of the Office of Assistant Chief Counsel (Income Tax and Accounting). For further information regarding this revenue ruling, contact Ms. Davis on (202) 566-4177 (not a toll-free call).

————————

APPENDIX B

Robert Neilson and Dorothy Neilson v. Commissioner
Tax Court Decision 94-1, 1990

Respondent's Deficiency Determination

During 1983 and 1984 petitioners operated a licensed day-care center in their home. Petitioners purchased their 3,000-square-foot home in 1981 for $119,624, of which $75,285 was allocable to the house. Eighty-nine percent of the 3,000 square feet of space was utilized for day-care purposes. The following schedules reflect the amount of deductions claimed by petitioners and allowed by respondent for the 1983 and 1984 taxable years:

In addition to the time children were actually present in petitioners' residence, petitioners spend about 2 hours each morning organizing the facility and preparing luncheon meals for the children. Petitioners also spent about one hour each evening after the children departed cleaning and reorganizing the day-care facility. Respondent did not consider the preparation and clean-up time in estimating 75 hours per week. Petitioners, on occasion, also provided day care on weekends. Respondent's formula did not consider the weekend use of petitioners' residence. Petitioners

Type of Deduction	Claimed in 1983	Allowed in 1983	Claimed in 1984	Allowed in 1984
Depreciation [2]	$5,057.00	$1,994.00	$5,057.00	$1,994.00
Lawn Care	532.00	- 0 -	608.00	- 0 -
Utilities	753.94	792.00	1,348.37	602.37
Repairs	960.00	442.90	- 0 -	- 0 -
Insurance	425.00	190.00	697.59	311.59
Real Estate Tax	1,369.44	611.44	1,464.29	654.29
Interest-Mtg.	5,455.17	3,171.17	7,035.85	3,912.86

Respondent determined that petitioners' use of their resident for day-care services was 75 hours per week. Respondent's estimate was based upon a log kept by petitioners that reflects the times and days that children were in petitioners' care.

utilized their residence for day-care business purposes for an average of 90 hours per week or 54 percent (90 divided by 168) of the ime.

Petitioners claimed and respondent disallowed $532 and $608 for lawn care in 1983 and 1984

[2] Petitioners claimed ACRS depreciation on the straight line method for a 15-year useful life. Respondent determined that only 89 percent of the residence was used for day-care purposes and that day care was provided for only 75 out of a possible 168 hours per week or 44.6 percent of the total time available for use. With the exception of the lawn care, which was disallowed completely, all other deductions were reduced to reflect the 89-percent and 75-hour factors determined by respondent.

Respondent concedes that any disallowed portion of real estate tax and interest would be deductible as "Schedule A" items. Petitioners concede that for 1983 the amount of interest claimed exceeded the amount they could verify and that they are therefore not entitled to $119 of the total deduction taken. Petitioners also concede that their personal use of the residence constituted 11 percent and, accordingly, only 89 percent can be considered for business purposes.

respectively, During 1983 and 1984 petitioners used the lawn areas around their residence for day-care business purposes. During 1983 and 1984 petitioners paid $532 and $608, respectively, for lawn care expenses, 54 percent of which is deductible in each taxable year.

Income Tax Deficiency–Merits

Generally, under section 280A, no deduction otherwise allowable shall be allowed with respect to the use of a dwelling unit which is used by a taxpayer as a residence during the taxable year. An exception to the general rule exists where the residence is used exclusively and on a regular basis as the principal place of business for any trade or business of the taxpayer. Sec. 280A(c)(1). Additionally, where a taxpayer uses a dwelling unit on a regular basis for day-care services, a deduction may be allowable based upon percentage of use. Section 280A(c)(4)(C) provides for a deduction in an amount equal to the expenses attributable to that portion determined by multiplying the total amount of the expense by a fraction, the numerator of which is the number of hours the portion is used for day care business purposes and the denominator of which is the total number of hours that the portion is available for use. Sec, 1.280-2(i)(4), Proposed Income Tax Regs., 45 Fed. Reg. 52399 (1980), amended 48 Fed Reg. 33320 (1983).

Petitioners bear the burden of proving the amount of their use and their entitlement to a deduction. Welch v. Helvering, 290 U.S. 111 (12 AFTR 1456) (1933); Rule 142(a). Initially, petitioners have conceded that 89 percent of their residence was utilized for day-care purposes and that 11 percent was used for personal use.

Petitioners maintained a log which reflected the name of the child, the date, and time spent at petitioners' residence. Respondent, based upon the log, determined that petitioners used their residence about 75 hours per week. Based upon petitioners' testimony we have determined that petitioners used their residence about 90 hours per week. Our finding is based upon that preparation and clean-up time which is not reflected on petitioners' log and upon the fact that petitioners occasionally provided day-care service on weeks. Respondent's determination of 75 hours per week is apparently based upon a 5-day week and 15-hours use per day. With 90 in the numerator and 168 in the denominator, petitioners would be entitled to 54 percent of 89 percent of the items claimed on their returns in connection with day care, except for the lawn care. The 89 percent limit does not apply to the lawn care because it appears that the children had exclusive use of that area during the time day care was being provided. Accordingly, 54 percent of the $532 and $608 claimed for lawn care in 1983 and 1984 respectively is allowable.

APPENDIX C

DEPRECIATION WORKSHEET

DESCRIPTION OF PROPERTY	MONTH/YEAR PUT INTO BUSINESS USE	PRICE*	BUSINESS USE % **	BUSINESS BASIS ***
HOUSE				
MAJOR HOME IMPROVEMENTS				
LAND IMPROVEMENTS				
PERSONAL COMPUTER				
ENTERTAINMENT, RECREATION OR AMUSEMENT ITEMS				
ALL OTHER PERSONAL PROPERTY ITEMS				

*Price: For all expenditures except the house, list the fair market value at the time of purchase or purchase price, whichever is lower. To arrive at the price of the house, take the purchase price minus the value of the land at the time of purchase. Add to this the cost of any major home improvements made before your home was used by your business.

**Business-Use Percent: For the house, major home improvements, land improvements and other personal property, use your Time-Space percentage or an actual business-use percent. For a personal computer and entertainment items, use an actual business-use percent, not your Time-Space percentage.

***Business Cost Basis: Multiply the Price for each item by the amount of the Business-Use Percent column. The Business Basis represents the amount you will be able to depreciate for each item. To find out how much of the Business Basis can be taken as an expense each year, see the *Family Child Care Tax Workbook.*

OTHER REDLEAF PRESS PUBLICATIONS

Business Receipt Book – Receipts specifically for family child care payments improve your record keeping; 50 sets per book.

Calendar-Keeper – Activities, family day care record keeping, recipes and more. Updated annually. Most popular publication in the field.

Child Care Resource & Referral Counselors & Trainers Manual – Both a ready reference for the busy phone counselor and a training guide for resource and referral agencies.

Developing Roots and Wings: A Trainers' Guide to Affirming Culture In Early Childhood Programs – The training guide for *Roots & Wings*, with 11 complete sessions and over 170 training activities

Family Child Care Tax Workbook – Updated every year, latest step-by-step information on forms, depreciation, etc.

Heart to Heart Caregiving: A Sourcebook of Family Day Care Activities, Projects and Practical Provider Support – Excellent ideas and guidance written by an experienced provider.

Kids Encyclopedia of Things to Make and Do – Nearly 2,000 art and craft projects for children aged 4-10.

The (No-Leftovers) Child Care Cookbook – Nutritional information and recipes to plan menus that children will eat for every day of the week, whether cooking for 1 or 100 children.

Open the Door, Let's Explore – Full of fun, inexpensive neighborhood walks and field trips designed to help young children.

Practical Solutions to Practically Every Problem: The Early Childhood Teacher's Manual – Over 300 proven developmentally appropriate solutions for all kinds of classroom problems.

Roots & Wings: Affirming Culture in Early Childhood Programs – A new approach to multicultural education that helps shape positive attitudes toward cultural differences.

Sharing in the Caring – Packet to help establish good relationships between providers and parents with agreement forms and other information.

Teachables From Trashables – Step-by-guide to making over 50 fun toys from recycled household junk.

Teachables II – Similar to Teachables From Trashables; with another 75-plus toys.

Those Mean Nasty Dirty Downright Disgusting but... Invisible Germs – A delightful story that reinforces for children the benefits of frequent hand washing.

CALL FOR A CATALOG OR ORDERING INFORMATION
1-800-423-8309